Quotes from Pam's students:

"Dr. Blackwell has helped me reach a part of myself I wasn't aware existed. At first, meditation was a great way to release tension and to gain a new renewal for life. Over time, I am realizing I am becoming a stronger, more centered and peaceful person with new abilities, like being able to be a strength to others."

—*Lyndsey V.*

"My husband passed away after a heroic battle with duodenal cancer. The meditative tools that Pam gave me helped him escape some of the pain and stress for a time. His favorite meditation was the walk up to the waterfall and then spending time behind the waterfall. I had him hold a smooth rock in his hand from a beach trip we took to the Oregon coast. We spent hours doing this, blessing Pam for sharing her talent with us."

—*Vickie S.*

"Pam's *Christ-Centered Meditation* has helped me quiet my mind and let the spirit illuminate my heart and mind. Her guided meditations of Christ are probably the most peaceful and fulfilling meditations I have ever participated in!"

—*Abel D.*

"...meditation brings me to powerful prayer, connection and sweet peace. Thank you, thank you, Pam. I have been so enriched by learning truths that have been woven into other cultures."

—*Donalee W.*

CHRIST-CENTERED MEDITATION

Handbook for Spiritual Practice

PAM BLACKWELL

Dedicated to my teachers and my students,
all of whom have brought me to joy

Cover Artwork: "Christ and Child" by Carl Bloch
Used by Permission
Cover design: Chris Trainor / trainorchris@gmail.com
Text layout: Brian Carter / briancarter.ut@gmail.com

Second Printing; December 2011
ISBN: 978-0-615-50255-7

Special thanks to my meditation students who have continually called for this book; to Cliff Mayes for his writing/editing support; friends and readers Stephen Nibley, Colin Forbes, Donna Nielsen, Karen Boren, Frank and Karen Horman, whose original idea on the 30-day contemplation exercise I borrowed. Thanks also to Joffrey Mehr, Nick DePalma, Marni Walker, and my daughter, Dana, and my soul-daughter, Liz, whose photographs are featured here.

Readers can offer their insights and share their meditative experiences at morningstarmeditation.blogspot.com or email the author at morningstarmeditation@comcast.net

Note: On each page of this book is something the Lord has said somewhere in scripture. His words are deliberately not referenced, chapter and verse, so that the reader can hear how He speaks without a specific filter. It is suggested you stop, say the words aloud, then allow yourself to bring to mind whatever associations or symbols may come... another way to ponder and come to know the Lord.

CONTENTS

PREFACE

Whosoever therefore shall humble himself
as this little child,
the same is greatest
in the kingdom of heaven.

—Matthew 18:4

I had the wonderful opportunity to see an exhibit of Carl Bloch's work. The Danish painter had a remarkable ability to translate some of the Gospel's most poignant moments into altar pieces, large paintings and etchings. I found I could only stay for just a few minutes. In the presence of such artistic mastery, the desire to actually be with Christ grew with each passing moment, and I left in tears. The last painting I stood in front of before leaving was "Christ and Child." I looked not only at Christ, but the child. To have His hand on *my* cheek. To have him point at *me*....

And as I try to convey the state of consciousness that being in the Kingdom of Heaven entails, I realize that this humbling, this stripping away of ego, is what I am try-ing to provide for the reader. Techniques I have experienced and teach—from Christian contemplative and Eastern

It is I; be not afraid

meditative traditions—all focus on leaving the conscious self, entering into child-like state, to merge into a oneness with God and Christ.

I have been wanting to write this book for nearly fifty years. When I was an undergraduate at Arizona State University in 1961, I was walking across the cafeteria when I was captivated by a poster and the face of an East Indian man. I copied down the address and information on the poster and sent away for meditation lessons by Parmahansa Yogananda, then deceased. I eagerly awaited my weekly lessons, alone in my enthusiasm for the effects of meditation in my young life.

Enter a Christian law student who had a band. We started hanging out together and through various spiritual conversations over months, I became an on-fire Christian. Then I wanted to teach what I knew about meditation to all my new Christian friends. The idea of incorporating Eastern meditation into traditional spiritual practice of prayer, fasting and church attendance was not well-received—not in 1967. The concept was so novel at that time.

After my studies, I moved to the San Francisco Bay area, where I was fortunate to study with Shunryu Suzuki-Roshi, who brought the practice of Zen Buddhism to the United States, and Tartang Tulku Rinpoche, who was sent to the U.S. by the Dalai Lama to introduce Tibetan Buddhism to Westerners. I studied tai chi in New Hampshire with an old Chinese teacher, Master Leung, who, though he did not speak English, embodied the physical and spiritual essence

Wilt thou be made whole?

of Taoism. I also meditated with nuns in the Netherlands in order to learn about the Christian contemplative tradition that stretches back to seventh century.

These widened my practice and exposure to the East especially, where individuals explored inner space, while we Westerners were busy analyzing and conquering the outer world.

When I felt I had experienced enough that I was ready to teach, I travelled through the United States and Europe leading meditation workshops beginning in the 1970s. Since that time, I have been fortunate to reach a wide audience with my love for the Christ-centered spiritual potentials of meditation.

Students have asked me time and again, "Where can I read about this?" "Why don't you write something I can use in my Christ-based practice?" I am pleased to have lived long enough that the times now allow Christians everywhere to incorporate the techniques of quieting the mind and opening to Spirit that I tried to offer so long ago.

—*Pam Blackwell, 2011*

I am the true light that lighteth every man that cometh into the world.

CHAPTER ONE

I remember the days of old.
I meditate on all your doings.
I contemplate the work of your hands.
—*Psalms 143:5*

WHAT IS MEDITATION?

The word "meditation" has increasingly entered popular speech over the last fifty years. Along with the popularizing of the term has arisen a popular image of the meditator. He or she is sitting in a lotus posture, arms extended and wrists resting on the knees, thumbs touching the tips of index fingers, eyes closed, and (after perhaps chanting a few mantras or phrases) attaining a state of blissful calm in which all of one's problems are almost magically solved as the person become perpetually calm and powerful. Although there may be some small elements of truth in this picture of someone who is meditating, it is, like most popularizations of profound ideas or practices, largely a misleading caricature of "the real deal." In fact, meditation means many different things to different people, depending upon the spiritual or

Set your troubled heart(s) to rest.

Lift up thine eyes round about and behold.

secular tradition within which it is practiced by those people. In this book, I will partly focus on the various spiritual traditions along with tried-and-true methods that I have culled from direct experience. My primary purpose in doing so is to help fellow Christians deepen their spirituality in thought, prayer, work, personal relationships, and service, and respond to our Savior's call to "Be still and know that I am God." (Ps. 46:10).

The Growth of the Western Interest in Meditation

Beginning in the 1960's, many people in the West started to become interested in the ancient meditative practices of the East. These Westerners were interested in it because of its potential to deepen and refine their spirituality.

The best example of this sort of dialogue between East and West on the topic of meditation was the correspondence between Father Thomas Merton and Dr. Daisetzu Suzuki. Father Merton was a Catholic priest, monk at the Abbey of Gethsemani, and an important poet of the 20th century. Dr. Daisetz Suzuki was the first scholar to bring the wisdom of Zen Buddhism to the West in work that he tailored to the Western reader.

One of the best fruits of their correspondence was Father Merton's book, *Zen and the Birds of Appetite*. Since that time, books and articles have proliferated and can be found in almost any well-known bookstore and in university libraries across the United States. A local university has over 3,200 books and articles on the topic of Christianity and Buddhist meditation, over 300 on Christianity and meditation in the Buddhist tradition, and over 200 on Christianity and meditation in the Hindu tradition. The partnership of meditation and a wide variety of religions, especially monotheistic ones, has been well established in various religious, scholarly and popular venues. It would seem just on the face of it that there are many ways that meditative practices can enhance one's walk as a Christian. And indeed there are many books, some scholarly and some for the layperson, that explore these potentials. Those books are all from either the Protestant and (especially) Catholic tradition. Until now, however, there has not been a book that offers a broad-based Christian meditation handbook that incorporates the best of what the East has to offer. This book is meant to fill that serious gap, and to do so in a way that brings the best of the author's studies, practices, and experiences to a Christ-centered individual in easy and enjoyable way, that will deepen his/her commitment to Our Lord Jesus Christ.

He that doeth truth cometh to the light.

The other group of Westerners fascinated by meditation beginning in the early 1960's has been psychotherapists. Alan Watts' book, *Psychotherapy: East and West*, is perhaps the earliest and still one of the best known works along this line. In this book, Watts, an Anglican priest and therapist, discussed how meditative practices can help us experience our internal processes more productively than we usually do.

My joy may be in you, and your joy complete.

He pointed out that, especially during times of psychological distress, we can use meditative techniques to experience (and eventually shape) our emotions in a more objective, detached, and even healthily impersonal way instead of being painfully tossed by them in an inner maelstrom of harsh judgments on ourselves and others, irrational terrors, and desperate clinging to that which cannot stay and is even in the process of departing as one clings. The meditative process of simply observing inner processes instead of trying to control them can "defuse" them—or can do so to a considerable degree. It is as if our emotions and thoughts somehow want to be coolly observed, and that, once they are, they stop clamoring for attention and just become what they are. When that happens, we can then experience them—pleasant, unpleasant, or both—and use them to gain greater balance in our internal and external lives.

And here is one of the delightful paradoxes and fruits of meditation: By not trying so hard to control what goes on inside of us, we actually gain more "control" over our inner life. As we, in an attitude of teachability, take an attitude of non-judgmental acceptance and curiosity about what goes on within us, we gain an increasingly clearer view of it and can therefore can become more "skillful" (as Buddhist monks put it) in using that energy for good, not being used by it as a helpless "victim."

In short, meditation in all of its many forms helps the practitioner learn to simply watch his or her inner dynamics without getting caught in them—like a quicksand pit of uncontrollable energies, which are equally uncontrollable whether they feel good or bad. "You are not your thoughts or emotions" is a motto of meditators everywhere. Rather, you are the eternal, calm, intelligent Center that wisely, dispassionately observes those ever morphing thoughts and emotions. Buddhist psychology pictures these perpetually shifting patterns of concepts and feelings within us as constantly changing clouds. Some are hopeful and sunlit, some are spooky and dark, and some are faint and hard to make out. But all of them have a hidden treasure of meaning within them if we will only let them be and approach them in curiosity and patience. When we do, we can then decide from and as our wise center, how close to them or far from them we choose to be, and what, if anything we wish to do with them, in faith, hope, charity, and action in the world.

I know my sheep and my sheep know me.

Another profession that embraced this import is the medical profession. In over 1,000 published research studies, various methods of meditation have been linked to changes in metabolism, blood pressure, brain activation, and other bodily processes. Meditation has been used in clinical settings as a method of stress and pain reduction.

When we examine the definition of meditation in various sources, we find several common elements:

1. Meditation is a "practice." As with most things that can make our lives better—physically, emotionally, intellectually, or spiritually—learning how to meditate and doing it more and more leads to every increasing benefits through practice. The more you do it, the better you become

Ask thee a sign of the Lord thy God; ask it either in the depths, or in the heights above.

at it, and the more inner riches and efficacy in the world it provides. Meditation is not a quick fix. It is a spiritual discipline.

Although "spiritual discipline" may sound daunting at first, it is really good news and something you can do! "A formal spiritual discipline?" a person might ask. "I don't have either the energy or the time for a formal spiritual discipline in my life! That's for monks, priests, and others. I'm busy enough taking care of my family and its thousand duties, working, not getting home until 5 or 6 p.m., and doing my hobby (if I can even find a few minutes for it), and trying to stay in some kind of physical shape so that I can do all of those things. Besides, why in the world could I ever practice something that monks devote their entire lives to in order to benefit from? If it takes them an entire lifetime of rigorous practice to get the benefit, it's not very likely that I'd get any benefit at all in the more limited way I could do it."

Although this response is understandable, it finally isn't correct. Here's why: Meditation is the original "gift that keeps on giving." We as meditators have found, just for starters, that when one meditates on a daily basis, even if for only a twenty minutes a day, it makes the rest of one's life much more clear, efficient, and compassionate. One's life just runs more smoothly in many delightfully surprising ways as one takes up meditation seriously. It is an investment of your time that pays big dividends—and bigger and bigger as one meditates more diligently. I am confident that you will find, as I have, that one gets much more done in the day—both inside oneself, outside oneself, and with others—the more one meditates in a day. To put it bluntly, every minute you put into meditation will get you two extra minutes (at least!). And those two minutes will be more peaceful, efficient, compassionate, and, yes, spiritual—no matter how mundane or maybe even unpleasant the activity you are engaged in—than they would have been if you had not done so.

That which is born of Spirit is spirit.

2. Meditation requires and develops "attention." We generally talk about "paying attention" to something or someone. It is important to be very clear about what I mean by "paying attention," for attention is crucial in meditation. In a very real sense, paying attention is meditation. Paying attention is directing one's mind or energies to something happening within or outside of oneself. When we pay attention, we expect or wait for something; and when it appears or occurs, we give heed to it, observe it closely. In this sense, meditation is active, not passive, as it is thought to be. Or rather, it is, paradoxically, and kind of passive action. In meditation, when something "comes up" in our flow of consciousness, we, from a quiet and detached center, focus upon it (the passive part) but we also stretch towards it (the active part), to see what that thing is—not necessarily as we would like it to be or fear that it might be.

Most of us live in this perpetual stream of mere experiencing second to second, minute to minute, hour to hour, day to day—even month to month, year to year, and for all

If I have told you earthly things, and ye believe not, how shall ye believe, if I tell you of heavenly things?

our lives. We feel that we are a small boat being tossed and turned in that ongoing stream of our internal events. The stream may be pleasant, unpleasant or neutral. But it's a stream that we feel we just exist within and, in many ways, just cannot control. If the boat that we call "ourselves" is floating along nicely, we say we are happy. However, just beneath the surface of those lovely waters is our fear that we will not be happy for long—that something or someone will come along to disturb our joy. Underneath each joy lurks the apprehension that it will go away. This causes us to cling.

This leads to anxiousness, even unhappiness, in the midst of joy. We, wanting to be in control, go running here and there looking for something that will provide us with a life of mere joy. We chase the illusion of joy like a cat its own tail. And because it is an illusion, our ongoing program of pure joy through control leads to pain. Indeed, control is not the solution. It is the problem.

Rather, by clearly, courageously looking at our present unhappiness or dissatisfaction straight on, we may learn from it what it is trying to teach us: Why we are unhappy right now? What does this unhappiness feel like in our bodies—what shifting patterns, locations, types and degrees of energy do we feel in our bodies in this unhappy state? What choices have we made to get us to this point? Or what have others done to us that has brought us here (so that we may maturely experience our justifiable anger or sadness because of it, and then healthily learn to forgive, love and move on, just as the Savior said)?

What is the solution to this dilemma? Is there a solution? I believe, along with two millennia of meditators from within almost every religious tradition and even from some non-religious ones, that the answer is to continue to develop oneself in meditative practices. For, when consciousness is viewed from the higher state of "super-consciousness," a detached consciousness that has been trained in meditation to see view our ordinary consciousness in a calm spirit of healthy curiosity, we then honor our inner events, each and every one of them. We can be like the Lord when He arose and said unto the sea, 'Peace, be still.' And the wind ceased, and there was great calm." (Mark 4:39)

I am the bread of life.

3. Meditation fosters a sense of well-being. By well-being, I do not mean always being happy any more than St. Paul seemed to have always been happy. I find throughout Paul's letters that he experiences and expresses the whole range of emotions. He is certainly happy at times. However, there are other times when he is sad, angry, confused, or even anxious.

However, there is no doubt that Paul, after his vision of the Savior and in his mission of spreading the Gospel of Jesus Christ, was a man who lived in a state of well-being. He had the full range of human emotions, and more than the typical range of adversities that most of us face. He felt those emotions fully, experienced adverse conditions

Except ye see signs and wonders, ye will not believe.

courageously, and expressed all of this in some of the most powerful words ever written.

Paul knew who he was, however, and was, I believe (and as the Quakers put it) quiet at the center. As he proclaimed, "not I live, but Christ lives in me." From that immovable center of peace, he was able to drink from the sweet foaming top of life's barrel of wine to its bitter dregs, and to live it beautifully for the sake of Christ. This is what a Christian life is, I humbly suggest: not avoiding the range of life's experience but bringing the mind of Christ—as best a mortal can do—to any and every situation.

My belief, and my reason for writing this book, is that meditation can help us reach that eternally peaceful center where Christ sets up his tabernacle inside of us and helps us wisely, powerfully, and compassionately live, so that, so that we allow Him to "…lead(eth) me beside still waters." From that center, the meditator may become more and more of a disciple of our Lord Jesus Christ every day, in any situation, and to the spiritual up-building of himself and with whom he interacts.

CHAPTER TWO

Let me understand
the teaching of your precepts!
Then I will meditate
on your wondrous works.

—Psalms 119:27

TECHNIQUES OF MEDITATION

Now that I have laid out the philosophy behind meditating, let me address the two types of meditation, which I call "active" and "passive." By "active" I am referring to guided meditation and work in dyads, which we will explain later in this chapter. "Passive" meditation involves meditators stepping back and observing the flow of thoughts that emerge as one sits quietly, or attempting to stop the flow of thought altogether. Here are the basics for "passive" meditation practice:

First, it is very helpful to find a place in your home where you can meditate that is quiet, where you will not be disturbed. If you can, early morning is the best time. Whenever you do it, don't practice on a full stomach. Although

The Son quickeneth whom He will.

many meditators sit in a lotus posture (seated with one leg overlapping the other), it certainly is not necessary. Definitely not do this if you feel that you will hurt yourself doing so. A chair is just fine. Just make sure you choose a sitting position that is both comfortable and allows you to sit with your neck and back in a straight position. Uncross your legs and place your hands on your thighs, either palms up or down.

Behold, thou art made whole.

Start with ten minutes; work up to twenty minutes. As I said in the first chapter, twenty minutes a day can provide profound physiological and psychological benefits. You may meditate with your eyes either open or shut: 1) Eyes open—look at a spot or an object (some use a lighted candle) or 2) Close your eyes, and let your eyes drift upward so that they are looking at point slightly above your eyebrows. (If you first start by pressing your finger in the spot, it is easier to find it with your eyes closed.)

Breath is very important in achieving a peaceful meditative state. Inhale from your diaphragm, in through your nostrils to the count of six; hold for six counts; then out through your mouth for six. Rest, then do that set for a total of six times. When you begin meditating, just allow the breath to flow, in a relaxed state.

Now, the hard part (but only at first!). In attempting to observe your thoughts, it is helpful to have something to do or say silently to yourself. You can count your in-breath up to the number ten. That is, you inhale and say to yourself, "One," then exhale. On the next inhale, you say. "Two," and so on until you reach the number ten, at which time, you begin again. If you lose track of the number you are at, no need to worry. Just begin again with "One." Some people keep track of the number by counting on their fingers. The value of this exercise is to give your conscious mind something to do while you let go of any thoughts that arise. Meditators often call this consciousness "the monkey mind" because we are always chattering inside our heads as if there were a monkey there just squawking on and on without saying anything useful, or indeed anything at all.

I have come in my Father's name.

Using a word or phrase which you repeat over and over as you meditate is another good way to attract the "monkey mind" and give it something to do. Your mind may resist this process; your job is to gently return to the "mantra" or phrase, so that you can come to experience an awakened spirit.

Common phrases are:

✳ <u>Be still and know that I am God.</u> (Psalm 46:10)

Peace, be still. (Mark 4:30)

Abba, Father (Mark 14:36)

Thy will be done. (Matt 26: 42)

✳ *Peace, I leave with you.*

With this second approach, you work to keep from thinking. The idea that we can stop conscious thought is surprising and novel. In the beginning, you learn to distance yourself from thoughts that arise by either imagining them as clouds, then wisps of clouds dissolving; or imagine that you see them on a white board and wipe them away.

Marvel not that I said unto thee, ye must be born again.

At first you may find that you can go ten seconds or so without thinking, but, as you practice, you experience longer and longer periods of quiet. With the quiet, you can achieve a state of calm where you can stop self-defeating "monkey chatter," and you can experience a profound physiological rest. In fact, it is only in a meditative state that you are fully relaxed. Your mind continues to drive you even at night. Even in times when you aren't dreaming in a non-REM state, your mind is still making grocery lists, insisting that you need to get a life and criticizing you for your choices. In an active dream state (REM) you are, for the most part, high speed problem-solving.

Active Meditation

"Active" meditation practice involves using imagination to cleanse, heal and reach higher states of consciousness. One of the most effective ways to "actively" meditate is to take a powerful dream that seems to have a spiritual charge to it and to imagine what happens after the dream ends. Carl Jung called this active imagination. Let us say that you dream that a Native American man appears in your dream to tell you something about an underground cave where treasure is buried. By sitting in a meditative state, with a note pad nearby, let yourself follow him into the cave and see what happens next. After you allow the "story" to unfold, then write notes. From the notes, you can extend this meditative state by drawing, painting or writing poetry about the experience.

What if you find that it is not easy to conjure up that Native American man—that you do not "see" or can imagine what happens. In order to activate visual imagery, try this exercise.

Imagery Exercise

Begin by looking for a few seconds at a candle flame. Now close your eyes and look at the bright after-image. Let this image become a bright-yellow sunflower with a brown seeded center and a long green stem.

The Lord formed me from the womb; yet shall I glorious in His eyes.

When that image is steady, move closer to the sunflower. Now imagine yourself diving into the center. Feel the rough seeds on your skin as you swim past them to the heart of the sunflower. Once you are in the center, find there a beautiful sun. Move into the sun and swim in the golden gases for a time. Feel the heat all over your body.

Finally, dive deeper into the sun until you come to a sunflower. Take a seed and eat it. This is a magical seed— as you eat, you can make a wish, and it will be granted. Ask to be taken home. Open your eyes and find yourself back. Take a moment to absorb the visual journey.

Light of Christ

Another way to meditate using the "active" modality is to imagine a white light coming down from above and entering the top of your head. Allow yourself to feel a warm, energetic and joyful feeling filling first the interior of your head, then slowly filling your shoulders, arms and hands. Let the light move in such a way that it pushes ahead of it any dark, gray, bruised parts out the palms of your hands.

Then, imagine the light slowly filling your chest, back, stomach, buttocks, thighs, calves and out the soles of your feet. Ahead of the light flows anything that needs to be discharged from your body. It is said that God has made the earth to take away any of our energetic refuse—that is one of the earth's functions.

To them that sit in darkness: Show yourselves.

Healing Heart

Because the Savior is the central figure in our spiritual culture, another "active" imagination exercise can involve imagining Him coming down from above. Imagine Christ coming down from the ceiling. Have Him stand before you and take your face in His hands. Look deeply into His eyes. See the love and affirmation of who you are coming from Him. Step back. Imagine taking your heart out of your chest. Examine the breaks and blows that it has endured. Then give it to Christ. See Him take your heart tenderly between His hands and send healing energy to it. See Him open His hands, and you see that you have a whole perfect heart. Insert it back into your chest. Put your hands over your heart. Feel what it feels like, now that it has been made whole. Express your gratitude to Him. Imagine Him returning upward until you cannot see Him any longer.

Tell Me Who You Are

Another "active" meditation involves working with two people. Sit opposite someone (couples: this is a really good exercise for you). Place your hands on your knees, right hand up and left hand down. Join hands so that your down-turned right hand is resting on your partner's upturned left hand. Repeat that on the other side. Breathe in for six counts, hold for six, then out for six. Allow yourself to "feel" the energy that goes out of your right hand and comes in the left hand. (Soon, you will just feel an even flow of energy going through both hands.)

Then, partner A says to partner B, "Tell me who you are." For five minutes, B speaks without being interrupted about anything that comes to mind. It does not have to be a speech that has been designed and constructed. It should just flow from one thought to another. Like, "I am a wife who loves Basset Hound puppies and sunsets. Ah…I am thrilled when I hear Rachmaninoff's Prelude in C Sharp Minor." When the five minutes is up, both of you say, "Thank you," to the other. Then it is A's turn. B says to A, "Tell me who you are." After five minutes, switch again, until you have each had four turns to talk. (This exercise gets harder and harder as you try to not repeat yourself, but it is useful to go deeper and deeper into one's consciousness and to witness that of your partner's.) When you are finished, take the time to say how you feel and what you have learned about the other.

Sing, O heavens; and be joyful, O earth.

CHAPTER THREE

My meditation of him
shall be sweet:
I will be glad in the Lord.

—*Psalms 104:34*

LEVELS OF CONSCIOUSNESS

To understand what it is to have joy, to live in a higher state of consciousness, it is important to look at the structure of psychological and spiritual growth. Many readers have been exposed to stage theories, such as those of Erickson, Piaget, Kohlberg (stages of moral reasoning) to Abraham Maslow's hierarchy of needs. He identified five layers of a pyramid which he labeled as: physical needs, safety/security, friendship and love, self-esteem, and finally self-actualization. His theory suggests that the most basic level of needs must be met before the individual will strongly desire (or focus motivation upon) the secondary or higher level needs. When he was a graduate student in New York City, he looked around at the highest functioning individuals he could access or study about and built his stage theory based

*Awake as in the
ancient days.*

Come with singing unto Zion.

on individuals who were at the top of their game, so to speak, in the corporate and entertainment worlds, along with celebrities, such as Albert Einstein, Jane Addams, and Eleanor Roosevelt.

Around the mid-1960s Maslow began to feel that his model, although correct as far as it it went, was incomplete. Above and beyond self-actualization needs, Maslow came to perceive the inherent human need to transcend oneself and to reach the "transpersonal" in order to make psychological contact with the "naturalistically transcendent and spiritual, and axiological (meaning ethical)." He called this religion with a little "r." One experiences this transcendence in epiphanic moments, or what Maslow termed "peak experiences." He realized his theory had not included such individuals as Mother Teresa, Gandhi, and others willing to risk all of those other needs for transcendent values and experiences. He then became a pioneer in establishing the field of transpersonal psychology, which is concerned with the study of humanity's highest potential, and with the recognition, understanding, and realization of unitive, spiritual, and transcendent states of consciousness. Without such contact with something higher than oneself as the center of one's psyche, one would, he said, eventually "become apathetic and ill."

Issues considered in transpersonal psychology include spiritual self-development, unitive and mystical states of consciousness. Within the transpersonal field, theorists have created stages of faith and spiritual growth, some borrowing from Eastern mediative systems the concept of seven stages of development.

Fowler's Faith Stages

First, let us look at perhaps the most well-known of the theorists, James Fowler. He outlined seven stages of faith development a person might go through as they mature through adulthood.

• Fowler's stages start with infancy, what he called Undifferentiated Faith. Here the infant develops basic trust with those providing for his/her care. This is characterized by being able to judge whether its environment is positive or not (i.e. warm, safe and secure vs. hurt, neglect and abuse). If consistent nurturing is experienced, one will develop a sense of trust and safety about the universe and the divine.

• At the next stage, when thought and language begin, the child opens up to the use of symbols in speech and play. In this stage, the child's imagination is formed. Here a child can be encouraged to use imagination to form a relationship with deity. But in this stage, reality is not well-differentiated from fantasy. For this reason, adults should be careful about teaching about the negative aspects of religion, like the devil and the evils of sin. This can harm a child of this age, leading him/her toward a very rigid, brittle and authoritarian personality as an adult.

• Fowler's third stage is called the Mythic, or Literal Stage. Here the child (or adult person stuck in this phase) is

Yea, I am he that comforteth you.

I am the Lord thy God, whose waves roared.

likely to start sorting out the real from the make-believe. Story becomes the major way of giving unity and value to experience, but the symbols in those stories are seen as one-dimensional and literal. Moreover, beliefs, moral rules and attitudes are also held literally. "If I follow all the rules, God will give me a good life."

• Next a person will normally move into the fourth of James Fowler's stages, the Synthetic/ Conventional stage around puberty. A great deal of research suggests that many adults never move beyond it. Here authority is located outside the self: in the church leaders, in the government, in the social group. Religious concepts are what Fowler calls "tacitly" held—that is, the person is not fully conscious of having chosen to believe something. Thus the name "Synthetic," which are beliefs, not the result of any type of analytical thought. Any attempt to reason with a person in this stage about his beliefs, any suggestion of demythologizing his beliefs, is seen as a threat. The name "Conventional" means that most people in this stage see themselves as believing what "everybody else" believes and would be reluctant to stop believing it because of the need they feel to stay connected with their group.

• When a person cognitively realizes that there are contradictions between some of his authority sources and is ready to actually reflect realistically on them, he begins to be ready to move to the fifth of James Fowler's stages. According to Fowler, it is ideal that a person reach this stage in their early to mid-twenties, but as noted it is evident that many adults never reach it. If it happens in the thirties or forties, Fowler says, it is much harder for the person to adapt. In Individuative/Reflective faith, the faith that the person never reflected about, and was not completely able to articulate the justification for, becomes filled with both a freedom that he now CAN reflect on it, and the burden that he now feels he MUST examine. The responsibility of this can be frightening but is necessary. At this stage faith requires that the person be willing to interrupt his reliance on external authority and relocate the source of authority within himself. Fowler calls this the formation of an "executive ego," which is not a bad thing. It just means the person is more able to govern himself without the need for rules from the outside. The strength of this stage lie in the capacity for critical reflection (and the willingness to face truths that may cause distancing from comfortable thought patterns and thus pain). But a weakness of this stage is that the person may put excess confidence in the rational, conscious mind, thus ignoring unconscious forces that become more prominent in the next stage.

Come with me, and I will make you fishers of men.

According to Fowler, when the person in Stage 5 becomes ready to attend to the "anarchic and disturbing inner voices" of the unconscious mind, he becomes ready to move on to Stage 6.

• The move to Stage 6 is unusual before mid-life. Here the person begins to expand his world beyond the "either/or" stance of the prior stage toward a "both/and" orientation where the answers (and the power of the rational mind to figure them out) are not so clear. People in this stage are willing to engage in dialogue with those of other faiths in the belief that they might learn something that will allow them to correct their own truths. Dreams and imagination are given credence. Meditation is very helpful to allow the individual to separate his Self/Soul from the voices of the conscious mind.

Blessed are those whose hearts are pure; they shall see God.

• The final of James Fowler's seven stages, Universalizing Faith, is reached only by the very, very few. Some religious systems call this state, enlightenment. They report feeling a fusion with deity. These individuals are able to sacrifice their own well-being for the greater cause. Such people may commit their total being to their identification with persons and circumstances where the futurity of physical or spiritual progress is being crushed, blocked or exploited. (And they often risk their own safety in order to help the helpless in unexpected ways.) These are the spiritual adepts who bless the lives of many, and who originate in many cultures world-wide.

Yogic Stages of Enlightenment

Another seven-stage system of classifying spiritual evolution comes from the yogic tradition. In it, spiritual individuals who can "see," describe seven whirling disks in the energy field of an individual, which the yogis call *chakras* or wheels. Starting at the base of the spine, Level one is characterized by attention to food, shelter, safety, connection with the body. Level two is seen at about an inch below the belly button. It represents the thoughts and ideas related to one's sexual identity as male or female, the drive to mate, to have children. In general, it is said to relate to our passion in life. From there Level 3, located at the solar plexus, represents our will or drive to succeed in the world.

Most religious traditions try to bring their believers to Level 4, which located at the heart center, at the middle of spine, adjacent to the heart. This center represents the ability to empathize, sacrifice for others and the ability to see and experience what another is thinking and feeling. Level 5, located at the throat, is characterized by a search to experience the real Self and then to express that truth. Often this is the energy center used by artists, poets, musicians. But it can represent any expression of one's soul or Self—a business or home decorating, for instance. There is also a feeling of wanting to withdraw from the mundane and a longing for higher spiritual experiences.

You have a rich reward in heaven.

The sixth level is located at a point between the eyebrows. It may be perceived as a ball of light with blue sparks or a dark, purple field of light with a golden halo. This is the level where dreams are produced, the paranormal is experienced and where the aspiration to contact with God or Christ or Buddha can be realized in vision.

Level Seven is sometimes referred to the thousand-petalled lotus—brilliant white and located where the baby's soft spot was. This is where meditators report feeling a merging of consciousness with God. One feels that he "knows" the mind of God and acts accordingly in a

transcendent state of awareness—always acting in a compassionate and selfless manner.

Temple in Israel

*Nothing shall be
impossible unto you.*

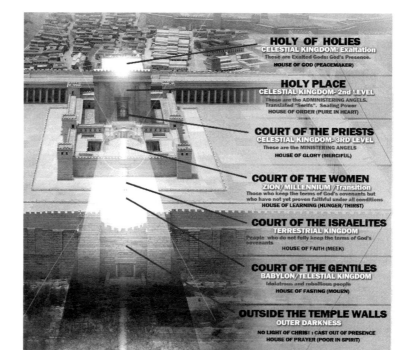

We can see these seven levels played out in the archi-
tecture of the Second Temple in Jerusalem. There were
seven gates and two veils, all perfectly aligned to 6.1
degrees north of due east. These faced the Mount of Olives
when the sun rose at its crest on April 6th. Starting from the
east and approaching the Temple on a line called "The
straight and narrow way" was,

   1) Outside temple walls—Outer Darkness, Poor in Spirit;

   2) Court of Gentiles—House of Fasting (Mourning);

3) Court of Israelites—House of Faith;

4) Court of Women—House of Learning;

5) Court of Priests—House of Glory;

6) Holy Place—House of Order; and

7) Holy of Holies—House of God, Peacemaker.

O woman, great is thy faith.

So we see that East and West both have models to help us understand where we are in our spiritual journeying. We are commanded by the Lord to follow Him to perfection. It is comforting to know that there is this seven-stage path that He walked, and that He stands at the end of it beckoning us onward and upward to rapturous oneness with Him. Although examining this continuum may diminish one's sense of spiritual importance, it does give a perspective that allows one to express gratitude for such individuals who have walked this path and to worship the Lord from a properly informed and appropriately reverent stance—on one's knees.

CHAPTER FOUR

Let every one of you so love his wife
even as himself; and the wife see
that she reverence her husband.

—*Ephesians 5:33*

MEDITATION FOR COUPLES

One of the best ways to enhance a relationship is to meditate. To spend twenty minutes in the evening meditating together is a quiet way to feel deeply safe and relaxed together. There are a number of ways to bring about these centered and safe feelings.

To begin, a couple needs to decide where they can dedicate a space that is quiet and undisturbed. This should be used on a regular basis, as the location begins to become part of a routine in which the body associates sitting in that location with relaxation and higher feelings of union and well-being. Lighting a candle or placing flowers or spiritual pictures in that location has the same effect.

Prayer should begin the meditation session. Often couples will use the beginning time, when they sit side by side,

A good man out of the good treasure of the heart bringeth forth good things.

to visualize members of the extended family as well, happy, whole. This replaces worry, which, in fact, sends negative energy to the person involved.

Exercise #1

It is given unto you to know the mysteries of the heavens.

Find a quiet place, where you can both relax. Sitting closely together in opposite chairs or in an Indian position in front of each other, place your hands on your thighs. Place your right hand on top of your partner's left hand (the other hand will be on the bottom). With this done, start a combined breathing exercise (try and match your breathing) with your partner. When ready, start visualizing the energy flowing throughout your body and then send this energy through one hand and receive your partners' energy through the other hand (like making a circuit). It does not matter how you visualize the energy flowing but as long as you allow your energy to flow out from you, into your partner, and allowing your partner's energy to flow into you.

Now with all this done, I would encourage you to start feeling the difference in the energy leaving your body and the one entering yours. What I mean by feeling is this:

- Physical sensation: Tingly, electric, heat (hands or all over), feel your heartbeat, sense your partner's heartbeat.
- Visualizing Sensation: If you can feel or see energy, what does the energy look like? Can you see your partner's energy flow?
- Emotional Sensation: Can you feel an emotion that you know is not yours, such as sadness, happiness, fear, joy?
- Spiritual Sensation: What kind of visions, voices, colors, sounds, smells and tastes are you experiencing?

Do this as long as there is an energy flow between both of you. Stop when you do not feel any flow from your partner. Share what you experienced with each other.

Thy King cometh unto thee.

Exercise #2

Sit opposite your partner. Sit close enough that you can stare into his/her eyes. As you do, say softly, "I have known thee of old." Say this for a couple of minutes, allowing yourself to let "memories" of the time before coming here to Earth to surface. It does not matter if it is "true" or not. Just let a story or stories unfold.

Then imagine a time when the two of you were in the presence of the Lord. Let that unfold.

Share your experiences and stories. A suggestion is to write these down in a spiritual journal which you two share.

Exercise #3

Because meditation can improve self-esteem and heal individual wounds, meditating together can allow the development of self-awareness that can lead to a heart-centered opening in the love relationship with one's self or one's partner. Meditation has been known to end arguments, get rid of grudges and clear the air between couples.

This exercise, from the yogic tradition, suggests that to begin, sit down opposite your partner; put your hands together in a prayer *mudra* (palms of the hands together with the base of the thumbs pressed against the sternum) and tune in to your sacred center. Look into your partner's eyes and bow your head in recognition of his/her Soul or Spirit. Project love from your heart and any other positive thought you like, such as, "We are a loving couple who seeks the Spirit of the Lord."

Bring yourself up sitting comfortably opposite your partner. Look into his/her eyes. Form your hands into a lotus (all the fingers are spread with the hands cupped). The male partner puts his little finger under the female partner's little fingers. These are the only fingers that touch. This makes the "heart lotus." Look into the soul, the heart, of

*Whatsoever is right
I will give you.*

your partner, through your eyes. Continue for one-and-one-half minutes.

Then place one hand over the other at your heart center. Close your eyes and meditate on your heart. Go deep within, to the center of your being. Continue for one-and-one-half minutes. To end, inhale deeply and exhale deeply three times, then relax.

Yogis and yoginis end their practice with either "The Sunshine Song" ("May the longtime sun shine upon you, all love surround you, and the pure light within you guide your way on") or you can sing one of your favorite hymns. Chanting and singing are good ways to bring your spirits together. The idea is to affirm the good work you have just completed and to bless yourself and others.

...pearl of great price...

Exercise #4

Find a comfortable place for you and your partner to meditate. If you want to play some music, there are many CDs with meditative music available. Sit back to back, whether it is cross-legged on the floor or on your bed. Wherever you choose to go, make sure that your backs are touching.

Feel your spines come together and take a nice deep breath. Let go of all thoughts.

Blessed are your eyes, for they see.

Close your eyes and start to synchronize your breathing, inhaling and exhaling together. Keep up with the synchronized breathing for a few minutes. You may want to start with the 6-6-6 breath for a total of six breaths. Then breathe normally, but together. Do this for about five minutes. Then pull your shoulders back about an inch and hook your arms together. Your left arm should be hooked into your partner's right arm, and your right arm should be hooked into your partner's left arm. Keep your breathing synchronized, at the start. Sway side to side together. As you move to one side, inhale together, and as you move to the other side, exhale together. Focus on slowly moving as one single unit. Do this for a few minutes.

Now, start to slowly move forward and backward. (As you go forward, your partner is moving back; and as you move back, your partner is moving forward.) As you move in one direction, inhale together; and as you start moving in the other direction, exhale together. Be sure to keep your arms hooked, and continue breathing together. Spend a few minutes doing this.

When you are finished, unhook your arms, and adjust yourselves so that you are both facing each other. Make eye contact, and as you do so, bring your breathing into harmony again. Keep this up for five minutes. It may feel strange to hold eye contact for this long, but it is worth it. You may feel any number of emotions coming up. You may feel like laughing or crying or talking. Do not respond. Just allow those feelings to flow through you and come back to center. After the eye-gazing and breathing, hug one another. Then sit back and gather your own energies and thoughts. When you are ready, share with your partner what you experienced. Many couples report this as a deeper way to make contact with each other that does not have to do with sex. In fact, in the yogic tradition there are many practices designed to help couples come to a sublime experience of a very high state of consciousness for both participants. When this happens, energy is aroused from the base of the spine and snakes its way up, from male to female sides to the top where both experience what they term *samadhi*, wherein the respective individual personalities and identities of each of the participants feel like they are completely dissolved in a unity of cosmic consciousness or union with God.

Arise, and be not afraid.

CHAPTER FIVE

"Unto Me?" I do not know you—
Where may be your House?
I am Jesus—Late of Judea—
Now—of Paradise.

—Emily Dickinson

CONTEMPLATION

Although contemplation can simply mean to attend to something exclusively, in this case we are talking about concentration on spiritual things as a form of private devotion, where we hope that we can come in contact with our Lord.

In order to do that, we usually think of choosing a particular passage of Scripture where we consider its meaning in our lives. We may look up cross-references to see what deeper meaning might be culled from this researching. In doing this, we are following a spiritual practice that goes back probably to the beginning with Adam and Eve. However, we do have a rather detailed expanded contemplative practice that was laid out by St. Ignatius in the 1500s, which

Where your treasure is, there will your heart be also.

D+C 6:23
Did I not speak peace to your mind concerning the matter? What greater witness can you have than from God.

*The lamp of the body
is the eye.*

consists of a 30-day focus on the life of Christ. It is on that system that this set of exercises has been adopted for this handbook.

These spiritual exercises of St. Ignatius of Loyola are a month-long program of meditations, prayers, and contemplative practices that help Christians become more fully alive in the presence of Christ. It presents a formulation of Ignatius' spirituality in a series of prayer exercises, thought experiments, and examinations of consciousness.

These exercises are usually made in one of three different ways: first, extended over approximately thirty days in a silent retreat away from home, which was its original form; or second, as condensed into a weekend; or third, in the midst of daily life, while living at home, over a period of a month's time. For most of us, the third is the only choice.

 Suggestions for 30-Day Contemplation

1. Make a commitment to read and study each lesson. Do them in order. There is never a time that is free of worldly demands and endless responsibilities. They will be there; you can and must take the time to both meditate and contemplate/ponder. If not now, when?

2 . Spend fifteen minutes on each day's activities.

3. Faithfully keep a log. Write at least one page per day. Write more if there is reason to do so. Leave enough time to do so.

4. If you miss a day, don't give up. Start with that day and continue.

5. Whatever time you set up to do this work, try to do it at the same time each day.

Enter by the narrow gate.

Thirty-Day Contemplation of Christ

Begin by writing what you think of Christ in your log.
Date the entry.

Day One

Question: How can I follow in His steps?

Read: 1 Peter 2: 9, 21

Ponder: How can I follow in Christ's steps today? In all my decisions, I will ask: What would Christ do? I will think of myself as a disciple of Jesus Christ.

Day Two

Question: Am I seeking Christ's help?

Read: Proverbs 3:5-6, 2 Corinthians 12:9-10

Ponder: Am I seeking the Lord's help in all I think and do? Do I pray enough? Do I pray with integrity? How can He help me overcome my weaknesses?

Day Three

Question: What do I need to do to be closer to Christ?

Read: Isaiah 55: 6, Heb 10:22

Ponder: What do I need to give up to be closer the Lord? What can I do to "remember" when I was with Him? List His personal characteristics.

Day Four

Question: Do I really love Christ?

Read: John 13:34-35, John 14:15

Consider the lilies of the field.

Ponder: Do I keep ALL the commandments or am I guilty of "selective" disobedience? Have I put another god before Christ?

Day Five

Question: Who am I really?

Read: Psalms 8:5-6, Isaiah 13:12

Ponder: What can I do daily to stay in touch with my "true" Self? How can meditation where I clear my mind of all thoughts help me find myself? Why does Christ care about me? In what ways do I see His hand in my life?

Day Six

Question: How can the Holy Spirit help me to be more like Christ?

Read: John 14:16-17, 26

Ponder: Do I really desire the Holy Ghost to be my constant companion? Do I listen and act when I hear the still, small voice?

Day Seven

Question: Do I believe in the Atonement of Jesus Christ for my sins?

Read: Luke 5:20-24, Ephesians 4:32

Ponder: Can I forgive myself for past mistakes TODAY? Can I forgive others who have done harm to me? How do I get rid of guilt?

Day Eight

Question: What is really happening when I take the sacrament?

Read: John 6:54, 1 Cor. 11: 26

Ponder: What promises have I made to Him? How will my life change if I truly take on His name?

Day Nine

Question: How do I guard against pride?

Read: Proverbs 6:16-17, Proverbs 8:13

Ponder: Am I being truly honest with myself? With others? Do I do the right things for the right reasons?

Day Ten

Question: Whom can I serve?

Read: Josh. 24:15, Gal. 5:13

Ponder: Am I overlooking family members, friends in order to serve in my church, my community? Or am I too focussed on family and not offering my skills to a wider

Truly, I tell you, nowhere in Israel have I found such faith.

community? What answers do I get when I pray to the Lord about this?

Day Eleven

Question: How do I control physical passions or addictions?

Read: 1 Cor. 10:6, 2 Tim. 2: 21-22

Ponder: How can I take my Savior's hand and rise to set a righteous example for others who also struggle? How can I build a spiritual network of support when I am tempted?

Day Twelve

Question: How can I stay in a grateful frame of mind for my many blessings for just one week?

Read: 2 Cor. 9:15, Eph. 5:20

Ponder: What ten things would I list as the most important blessings I have received from my Savior?

Day Thirteen

Question: How can I elevate my thoughts? Find a mountain of dispassion to climb and rest on?

Read: Ps. 119:99, Ex. 26: 30, 34

Ponder: Do I really want to work to keep all idle, unclear or negative thoughts out of my mind? Am I willing to discipline myself to practice meditation techniques to rid myself of these?

Set your mind on God's kingdom.

Day Fourteen

Question: How can I withdraw my negative projections from individuals and institutions, so that I do not gossip or think negative thoughts about them?

Read: Matt 5:11, Prov. 21:23

Ponder: Do I project onto the world my own unfinished or unresolved issues? What can I do to work on them? Can meditation help with the detachment necessary to accomplish this task? Should I get counseling help to accomplish this?

As you have believed, so let it be.

Day Fifteen

Question: How can I forgive someone who has really betrayed me or hurt me?

Read: Col 3:12-17. Matt 5:44

Ponder: Am I enjoying at some level the negative feelings that this hurt has provoked? Do I want to hang on to them and seek revenge? Could my self-condemnation preventing me from coming to Christ?

Day Sixteen

Question: Am I valiant in my belief of Christ?

Read: 2 Tim. 1:7, 8, Rev. 12: 10-11

Ponder: Do I counter negative comments about Christ? Do I speak of the teachings of Christ in the company of non-believers? When asked, am I ready with my testimony of the Church?

If your eyes are sound, you will have light for your whole body.

Day Seventeen

Question: How do I know my Heavenly Father loves me?

Read: John 3: 16-17, 1 John 4: 7, 10, Jeremiah 31: 3

Ponder: Do I project the negative feelings I have for authority figures onto my Heavenly Father? Do I seek Heavenly Father in prayer and ask to feel His love and counsel?

Day Eighteen

Question: What is the pure love of Christ?

Read: 1 Cor 13: 1-4, John 10:9

Ponder: Am I willing to live in a greater and deeper state of happiness and joy? Am I willing to discipline myself spiritually, so that I experience the pure love of Christ on a daily basis?

Day Nineteen

Question: How can I recognize Lucifer's enticings in my life?

Read: Rom.16:18-20, Luke 22:31

Ponder: Being in constant contact with the Lord is the strategy that keeps Lucifer and his minions from bothering me. Do I recognize the pattern of discouragement and enticement as part of his campaign? Am I willing to fully resist?

Day Twenty

Question: Do I spend as much time learning about the Savior and meditating on His words as I do watching television or involved in other electronic media?

Read: Romans 10:14, 2 Peter 1:3-9

Ponder: What books about the Savior and His teachings could I read this year to increase my knowledge? Will I search for ones that interest me, so I have the desire to read it? Am I willing to share what I learning with a friend or family member who may want to read the same book at the same time?

Surely life is more than food.

Day Twenty-One

Question: How can I resist being envious of the success and belongings of others?

Read: Rom. 13:13, 1 Tim. 6:4

Ponder: Do I realize that I have a spiritual purpose in this life? If so, what am I doing to pursue that path?

Day Twenty-Two

Question: How can I be sure that friendships with married people of the opposite sex are just that and not adulterous?

Read: 1 Tim. 5:11. Prov. 6:32

Ponder: If I am married, am I working to make my relationship satisfying for both of us? ~~If I am single, am I pursuing relationships in a Christ-like manner?~~

Day Twenty-Three

Question: How can I be a peacemaker?

Read: Mark 5:34, Col. 3:15

Ponder: Do I act as mediator with family members who are having difficulty getting along? Do I go around at a low "boil" most of the time? Do I hold grudges?

Tomorrow will look after itself.

Day Twenty-Four

Question: Am I truly changing the way I think and act as I strive to become more like Christ?

Read: Eph 3:16-19, Matt 6:21

Ponder: Am I experiencing a mighty change of heart? Am I clearing my mind with meditation and listening for His voice? Am I taking action when I do hear His voice?

Day Twenty-Five

Question: If I believe in the Second Coming of Christ, what am I doing to prepare for the Lord's return?

Read: Matt 24: 42, 46

Ponder: What changes do I have to make in order to be ready for the Second Coming? Am I willing to entertain the thought that His return may be in my lifetime?

Day Twenty-Six

Question: How can I help from becoming discouraged when I fall short of my spiritual goals, such as controlling my temper or being judgmental or negative about those around me who are striving to live Christ-like lives?

Read: Matt 6:1-15, Titus 2:14

Ponder: Do I believe that I can be perfected through Christ? How can that happen?

Day Twenty-Seven

Question: Can I imagine the tender look of love in His eyes when Christ says my name and reaches out to hold my hand, when I "knock" as He has commanded?

Read: Luke 11:9, Rev. 3: 20

Ponder: If He is just on the other side of the door, why don't I knock more often? What is it to entertain the presence of the Lord? How can I prepare myself for the real meeting with the resurrected Lord?

The very hairs of your head are numbered.

Day Twenty-Eight

Question: As I read about His life in scriptures, how do those incidents resonate with me?

Read: 1 Cor 14: 1, John 13: 15

Ponder: What patterns of the Lord's life are those I would and could emulate as I walk in His footsteps right now in my life? What characters do I identify with? Why?

Day Twenty-Nine

Question: How have I changed this month as I have searched myself in relation to Christ and His example?

Read: John 17:3, 11:25-27, 14:6

Ponder: Can I set my spiritual sights higher? If so, what particular steps do I want to take?

Day Thirty

What went ye out into the wilderness to see?

Write what you feel about Christ now that 30 days have passed. Compare what you wrote with your first entry.

Read: Isaiah 40:5, Ps. 119:24

Ponder: What is most precious in my life?

CHAPTER SIX

If you put your conditioned intellect
to rest for a long time,
suddenly it will be like the bottom
falling out of a bucket—
then you will naturally
be happy and at peace.

—Yauwu

OTHER SPIRITUAL PRACTICES

Zen Buddhism

Zen is a particularly austere form of Buddhism that developed in Japan in the 8th-century and continues to be practiced both there and around the world by increasing numbers of people. A great deal of Buddhist theory and many of the meditative practices that have become so well known in America over the last 60 years stem from the Zen branch of Buddhism.

As already mentioned in earlier chapters in the discussion of meditation, Zen also counsels us not to get too attached too—or tied up with—any mental formation or

Come unto me, all ye that labour and are heavy laden, and I will give you rest.

Ye shall find rest in your souls.

emotional impulse that may be controlling us at any given moment. It similarly advises us to look with a similar equanimity at whatever is going on outside of us. Whatever is happening inside or outside of you or me will inevitably pass. All things do—good, bad, or neutral (or, what is much more common, a mixture of all three!). That is just the nature of our experience as human beings, and nothing can change that. Least of all, it seems, will God deprive us of the benefit of experience in all its complexity. For it is through this that he forges us into wiser priests and priestesses in our daily ministries that we perform in His name and for His purposes (which we usually only dimly see) as we simply go about our days, living our lives. Zen "detachment" from the overheated ups and downs of our minute-by-minute (and sometimes second-by-second!) experiences of what is happening within and without us helps us not get caught up in that flux. The flux of impressions, sensations, hopes and fears that beset us at any given moment too easily blurs our vision, causes us to think irrationally, leads us to interact with others (especially those we most love) either too firmly or not firmly enough, and, in general, decenters us so that we do not make good decisions for ourselves and others.

That famous "Zen detachment" that has entered popular speech is real, and it is really helpful. When our practice in meditation—watching things rise and fall, evaluating them more intelligently, and deciding what we wish to do or not do about something, before we let it go and slip away into the flow again—becomes our practice in our everyday awareness, then we get a sense of the lovely Zen idea that "enlightenment" is nothing more than your everyday, ordinary mind, going about its business, big and small, in clarity and compassion, being a blessing to others and to oneself, and moving into deeper understanding of what it means to walk like the Savior did—and does.

✳ *Exercise—Walking Meditation*

Like the lamp, you must shed light among your fellows.

1. When you begin walking meditation, there is only one thing you have to do: be mindful of the act of stepping while you silently say, "Stepping, stepping, stepping," or "left, right, left, right." Walk at a slower speed than normal during this practice. Ideally this occurs outside, preferably in nature.

2. After you have practiced this several times, then add, "Stepping, putting down." You try to be mindful of the two stages in the step: "Stepping, putting down; stepping, putting down."

3. When you've practiced this for awhile, then you try to be mindful of three stages: (1) lifting the foot; (2) moving or pushing the foot forward; and (3) putting the foot down.

4. Finally add four stages in each step. Be completely mindful and make a mental note of these four stages of the foot's movement: "Lifting, moving forward, putting down, pressing the ground." At first you may find it difficult to slow down enough to perceive the four stages, but as you

pay close attention to all of the movements involved, you will automatically slow down.

5. To add a meditative mantra to this exercise, while you take two or three steps for each in-breath and each out-breath, breathe in and say, "I have arrived;" breathe out and say, "I am home."

Another mantra is to breathe in and say, "In the here;" and to breathe out and say, "In the now." A third option is to breathe in and say, "I am solid;" and breathe out and say, "I am free." A fourth option is to breathe in and say, "Lord Jesus Christ;" and breathe out while saying, "Have mercy."

As you carry on this practice, you will likely observe much more. When you lift your foot, you will experience lightness of your foot. When you push the foot forward, you will experience the movement from one place to another. When you put the foot down, you will feel the heaviness of your foot, because the foot becomes heavier and heavier as it descends. When you put your foot on the ground, you will feel the touch of the heel of the foot on the ground.

As you walk, look around and see how vast life is, the trees, the white clouds, the limitless sky. Listen to the birds. Feel the fresh breeze. Life is all around us, and we are alive and healthy and capable of walking in peace. Let us walk as a free person and feel our steps get lighter. Let us enjoy every step we make. Each step is nourishing and healing. As we walk, imprint our gratitude and our love on the earth. As we walk, let us be aware of the Spirit infusing us with the love of our Lord.

First go and make your peace with your brother.

Taoism

Taoism is considered to be the oldest of the world's major religions, dating back to about 3000 B.C.E. It was founded by a great sage named Lao Tzu. He wrote *The Tao Te Ching*, which some Western readers may be familiar with, especially its popularization in the delightful little book, *The Tao of Pooh*. Lao Tzu's disciple, Chuang Tse, wrote many commentaries on his master's work. Although there are various volumes that contain both of these great wise men's writings, my favorite is the translation by Lin Yutang.

The basic principle of Taoism is that the Divine goes far beyond anything I could say about it in ordinary language. Poetry comes closer (and that is why Lao Tzu wrote in poetry, one imagines), but even poetry is not adequate to capture the Infinity of the Tao, or God. For that is how the earliest Catholic missionaries to China, reading *The Tao Te Ching* and seeing much in it that was consistent with and prefigured the Gospel, translated the word *Tao* into God. We often say that the ways of God are mysterious. Isn't this really saying just what the Tao Te Ching asserts? God is the ultimately transcendent Being. We know some things about Him that have been given to us through revelation, anciently and recently. We are profoundly grateful for such knowledge. But if we think that that is all there is to know about God, then we are effectively trying to "corral" the Infinite within the tiny circle of our very finite, very limited

It is right for us to do all that God requires.

understanding. This is why Lao Tze wrote, "He who speaks does not know. And he who knows, does not speak."

Taoism puts its complete faith in the belief that God (or the *Tao*) will ultimately work everything out if we just let Him (or It). The more we try to second-guess God, frantically running here and there for solutions and not just resting in prayer and then humbly following the direction that the Spirit naturally takes us in answer to our prayers, we then end up making matters worse. As the saying goes, "The road to Hell is paved with good intentions." Therefore, Taoism prizes what it calls *Wu Wei*, or "inaction," but this does not necessarily mean doing nothing. It means being meditative, growing calm and centered, listening to the still small voice of that Self at the core of our being which is where Christ resides, and letting the Spirit guide us in Its timely and appropriate way.

Another interesting feature of Taoism is how it envisages the ultimate nature of the Divine. Again, the reader will recognize these terms from Taoism that have fallen into common speech (and usually in a way that does not reflect a deep understanding—sometimes not even a shallow understanding)—of what the terms originally and truly mean. The two terms I am referring to are Yin and Yang. The Divine Power, says Taoism, is really a harmonious interaction of two distinct but equal and unified forces.

Yang is the masculine aspect of Divinity. It is forceful, penetrating, shaping, and irresistible when it arrives, and, if left to operate unhindered without puny human meddling, is

There must be no limit to your goodness.

the full "power of heaven," which is also how Yang is some-times translated.

Yin is the feminine aspect of Divinity. It is that in the universe which is calm, receptive, that opens itself up to receive the essence of the masculine principle so that it can be fertilized by it and thus bring forth new fruit. It is the Great Mother, without whom the Great Father could do nothing, for He would have no way of being fruitful. Fruit-fulness is the essence of the Great Mother, patience, organic rhythms and periodicities.

It is the goal of Taoism to find a balance of these two, to operate from the Middle Way.

When you pray, go into a room by yourself and shut the door.

Tai Chi—Moving Meditation

Tai chi developed in ancient China. It started as a mar-tial art and a means of self-defense. Over time, people began to use it for health purposes and meditation as well. Accounts of the history of tai chi vary. A popular legend credits its origins to Chang San-Feng, a Taoist monk, who developed a set of 13 exercises that imitate the movements of animals. He also emphasized meditation and the concept of internal force (in contrast to the external force empha-sized in other martial arts, such as kung fu and tae kwon do).

There are many different styles of tai chi, but all involve slow, relaxed, graceful movements, each flowing into the next. The body is in constant motion, and posture is impor-tant. The names of some of the movements evoke nature (e.g., "Embrace Tiger, Return to Mountain"). Individuals practicing tai chi must also concentrate, putting aside distracting thoughts; and they must breathe in a deep and relaxed, but focused manner.

Native American Spiritual Practice

The kingdom of heaven is at hand.

When one thinks of a Native American medicine man, he or she often thinks of an old man shaking a rattle over a sick brave. Although tending to physically ill individuals was certainly a part of the medicine man's art, as with many Americans' ideas about Native Americans, this one is largely based in movie images and is at best very incomplete.

To begin with, medicine men were not always men. There were medicine women, too, and there still are. Furthermore, medicine men/women do not only deal with physical ailments. They deal with emotional and spiritual problems primarily, for even physical problems were seen as, at root, a result of a deeper imbalance in the patient's relationship with Spirit.

In the world view of Native Americans, the sun and the earth are considered to be metaphorically parents of all organic life. From the sun comes the quickening principle of nature, and in the patient and fruitful womb of the mother are hidden embryos of plants and men. Their reverence and love for nature is an extension of the love they feel for their parents and family.

The elements and majestic forces in nature, such as lightning, wind, water and fire are regarded with awe as spiritual powers. They believe that the spirit pervades all creation, and that every creature possesses a soul in some degree.

From his/her mother's breast, a child is taught spiritual lessons. Birth is considered to be a woman's greatest contribution to the world. Her child is considered mysterious, holy.

She brings her spiritual teaching to the breast. She points an index figure to nature; then in whispered songs, bird-like, at morning and evening, she shows the child that birds are real people, who live very close to the 'Great Mystery.' The murmuring trees breathe His presence, the rustling brook chants His praise.

If the child should start to be fretful, the mother says, "Hush, hush, the spirits may be disturbed." She diverts his/her attention to the voice of the aspen or the night's skies. Silence, love, reverence—these are first lessons. Later on, she adds generosity, courage and chastity.

There is one overarching duty, that is the duty of prayer—the daily recognition of the Unseen and the Eternal. Morning begins with prayer to the rising sun. If one comes upon a strikingly beautiful scene in the daily travel, he/she pauses for a moment of worship. All days are holy and set apart for the worship of God.

Some children display unusual spiritual propensity early. They are often taken by the medicine man or woman

He hath ears to hear, let him hear.

for specific training. There are sacred ceremonies that are passed down to the next generation to help restore harmony and vitality in the world and within individuals.

Medicine men/women use their connection with Nature's spiritual energy to balance individuals and the tribe. They receive their calling in the form of dreams or open visions that inform them that this is to be their destined path in life. It is a call that the soon-to-be initiate often resists, because it means that the young person will probably have to experience a great deal of pain in life, so that he/she will know how to empathetic to others in pain.

For my yoke is easy, and my burden is light.

He/she is taught to journey both to the underworld and the heavens, serving as what is called in Jungian psychology a "psychopomp"—a word that comes from the combination of the word for "soul" and "guide." A medicine man/woman guides others in their spiritual journeys and uses herbs that have proven to possess healing powers, if needed.

Chanting and drumming

There has been quite a bit of interest and research into creating the "shamanic" states that the medicine man/woman is able to slip into. One of the brain research findings is that the rhythmic beat of 4.5 beats per second produced by repetitive chanting and drumming creates theta brain waves. When we create theta, we fall into a very relaxed state.

A number of companies, both musical and research, offer CDs which help the meditator experience extended states of alert relaxation. One I know of personally is Joe Fire Crow who is a Northern Cheyenne flutist, Grammy nominee and flute-maker whose recordings include chanting and flute-playing. His recordings can be found at: josephfirecrow.com

Nature Symbols Exercise

I will put my spirit upon him.

Medicine men and women look for signs in Nature to help with their own and others' healings. This is an exercise using nature symbols to explore your own fear.

This exercise is to be done outdoors, if possible. Consider each of the following questions one at a time in sequence. Holding the first question in your mind, walk in any direction that you feel inclined. Then notice what object(s) first attract your attention and it (them) down in the space under question number one.

Now read the second question and again move in whatever direction you feel like you would like to walk. Notice what now attracts you as you repeat the second question to yourself.

Repeat the same process for the remaining two questions. Leave yourself open to the experience before you try to analyze what it may mean.

Now read the first question along with natural symbol answer. Talk to yourself about what the symbol means to you. How does it relate to the first question. Do the same for the other three. See if there is a pattern to the way the symbols have presented themselves.

According to thy faith, be it upon you.

1. What fear is blocking me from moving forward in my life?
2. What belief do I need to change to drop this fear?
3. What step(s) do I need to take to change this belief?
4. How will dropping this fear bring me closer to the Lord and change my life?

Check out how you feel about the exercise. Sit and meditate for a few minutes and see what may come to mind. Decide what realistic actions you can take in light of this "revelation." Promise yourself you will act.

Tibetan Buddhism

Buddhism was imported from India in 700 A.D to Tibet. The worship includes reciting prayers and intoning hymns, often to the sound of great horns and drums. A protective formula of spiritual significance, *Om mani padme hum* [*Om*, the jewel in the lotus], is repeated; it is inscribed on rocks and walls, tallied on prayer wheels, and displayed on banners and streamers. In addition to a large pantheon of spirits, demons, and genii, many Buddhas and *bodhisattvas* (future Buddhas) are worshipped along with their ferocious consorts, or Taras. Before the invasion of the Chinese beginning in 1949, about one is six men were monks. The country was filled with beautiful monasteries, most of which have been destroyed by the Chinese.

The most dedicated Tibetan Buddhists seek *nirvana*, which is defined as a state of supreme liberation and bliss, contrasted to samsara or bondage in the repeating cycle of death and rebirth. The word in Sanskrit refers to the going out of a flame once its fuel has been consumed; it thus suggests both the end of suffering and the cessation of desires that perpetuate bondage. They believe that *nirvana* is attainable in this lifetime. This phrase has often been interpreted as "annihilation," but in fact the Buddhist scriptures say that the state of the enlightened man cannot be described.

Certainly the most famous Tibetan is the Dalai Lama, known as a man of peace. In 1989 he was awarded the Nobel Peace Prize for his non-violent struggle for the liberation of Tibet. He has consistently advocated policies of non-violence, even in the face of extreme aggression. He also became the first Nobel Laureate to be recognized for his concern for global environmental problems.

The appeal of Tibetan Buddhist practice to Westerners has been the ability of their monks to demonstrate that happiness is something we can cultivate deliberately through mental training that affects the brain. In well-publicized study, Tibetan Buddhist monks came to the University of Wisconsin at Madison. The first subject to be studied was the abbot of a monastery in India who had practiced meditation, particularly compassion meditation, for over thirty years. After being fitted with an EEG skein of 256

Thou shalt have treasure in heaven.

electrodes, he was asked to alternate neutral mental activity with six mental states, including compassion meditation. When asked to demonstrate this form of meditation, the gamma waves emitted from his left frontal lobe were higher than 99.75 of anyone ever measured. And in the resting periods between meditations, the gamma signal never died down. The left frontal lobe is the one attributed to joy and feelings of well-being. What is suggested in this pioneering study is that we can alter our happiness set point.

You shall do homage to the Lord your God and worship him alone.

Compassion Meditation Exercise #1

To begin, assume a comfortable position. You may want to sit in a chair or on cushions on the floor (just make sure your back is erect). Take a few deep, soft breaths.

Close your eyes or leave them slightly open and begin by thinking of someone you care about—perhaps someone who has been good to you or an inspiration to you. Visualize this person or say his/her name to yourself. Get a feeling for his/her presence and silently offer phrases of compassion for him/her. The typical phrases are: "May you be free of pain and sorrow. May the Spirit of peace. May you be well and happy." But you can alter these, or use others that have personal significance.

Then move on to someone you find difficult. Get a feeling for the person's presence, and offer the phrases of compassion to that individual. Say them over and over, even if you don't feel compassionate.

Then turn your attention to someone you have barely met—the supermarket checkout woman or a new person at church. Even without knowing his or her name, you can get a sense of the person, perhaps an image, and offer the phrases of compassion in their direction.

Now offer with compassion to people everywhere, to all forms of life, without limit, without exception: "May all beings be free of pain and sorrow. May all feel the peaceful presence of the Spirit of the Lord. May all be well and happy."

Love your enemies and pray for your persecutors.

Close with shifting your attention inward and offering the phrases of compassion to yourself: "May I be free of pain and sorrow. May I feel the Spirit of the Lord who brings me peace. May I be well and happy." Repeat those over and over for several minutes.

Compassion Meditation, Exercise #2

Sit erect. Take several deep breaths. Close your eyes. Imagine a beam of white light coming down from above and entering into the top of your head. This light beam exudes joy and energy. Allow it to filter down into your neck, then down your chest until it comes to a place in the middle of your chest next to your heart.

Allow the beam of light to emerge from your chest toward the world which you can see in front of you. It is as it is seen from space. A beautiful blue and white ball. Allow the beam to cover the earth while you feel the love that comes in from above and is carried on this beam through

You are salt to the world.

your heart, covering the whole earth and every living being on it. Feel yourself as the conduit for the Spirit toward all mankind. Sit for several minutes allowing this passage to occur.

CHAPTER SEVEN

I have more understanding
than all my teachers;
for Thy testimonies
are my meditation.

—Psalms 119:99

MORE MEDITATION FOR COUPLES

In this busy world, it is hard for a couple to find the time to be together in a non-verbal, spiritual way. In Exercise #1, taken from a Sufi practice, the focus is on allowing yourself to see your spouse as the Beloved—seeing past the hurts and limitations that are part and parcel of being human—into the soul of the one you love—your Beloved.

I am the beginning and the end.

Exercise #1

Set a timer and just breath together, which is a delight. Feel your Beloved's gaze on your eyes. Know that your Beloved is breathing for you, is breathing a vital life force into and through you, as you are breathing for your

Beloved. Every breath in and every breath out is providing the gift of life for your Beloved.

Then, refocus your breathing. Together you are now breathing for everyone you know and love. Then together you are breathing for the whole planet.

Return to breathing for your Beloved. Feel your Beloved breathing for you. Then let there be just one breath—it is Christ's Breath.

Behold, mine arm of mercy is extended towards you.

Exercise #2

This is a very quick way to establish a beautiful heart connection with your Beloved spouse. (This is also taken from the Sufi tradition.)

Sit or stand facing one another, about two feet apart, and close your eyes. Take two long breaths, in and out to the count of six.

Open your eyes and gaze silently into the eyes of your Beloved. (If you open your eyes first, wait for him/her to open his/her eyes, while you gaze upon them with love.)

Continue to gaze silently into one another's eyes for several long breaths, in and out. Then close your eyes again. (If your Beloved closes his/her eyes first, then you close yours.) With your eyes closed, imagine that your Beloved is still gazing at you. Let your Beloved see into your heart center, located in the middle of your chest, the place protected by your rib cage.

Allow your own breath to fill your heart. When you open your eyes again, and you see into your Beloved's eyes, imagine that not only your eyes are connected but also your hearts.

Continue to gaze into one another's eyes for several long breaths, in and out. Repeat.

Each time you close your eyes, imagine that you are inviting your Beloved to see into your body. Move your inner attention upward to the top of your head. Then let your inner eye move slowly downward from your eyes, throat, heart to your belly, then your thighs, all the way down to the soles of your feet. Let the feeling of being totally open to your Beloved permeate you.

Each time you open your eyes, maintain eye contact with your Beloved, and breathe. Notice how the heart connection between you continues to grow stronger.

I will give unto the children of men here a little and there a little.

Exercise #3

Sit opposite each other. Lay right hand on upturned left hand. Take several long breaths. Allow the energy to flow between you. Then imagine a beam of white light is slowly descending from above. As it approaches the top of your head, let the image of Christ emerge. Imagine He comes down to stand between you. He looks first into the man's face, then the woman's. See the love and wisdom in Christ's face. Imagine that He walks behind the man and places His hands on his head. Feel the weight of His hands and the energy that flows from Him to you. Listen as He pronounces a blessing that will enable you to continue your commitment to being the best partner you can be.

Repeat the blessing for the woman. Then hear Him say that He is a third partner in this blessed marriage, always available to help at any time. Then let His image merge with the light and flow upward. Open your eyes, look at your Beloved for a moment, then share what you saw and heard.

Exercise #4

Whosoever shall compel thee to go a mile, go with him twain.

Here are the steps for an intimate experience of spirit with your loved one. Sharing spiritual intimacy transforms your relationship into a love affair that invites the Holy Spirit to bring you to higher states of consciousness—together.

Choose a location that is quiet and private. Create a supportive environment by using candles. Keep it light enough to see each other's eyes. Play relaxing music very quietly in the background. Another alternative is to be outside in nature.

You can sit on the floor, meditation style, or use two chairs facing each other. Place a pillow across your laps so that you can comfortably reach each others' hands. The goal is to have your backs comfortably upright, with your faces and hearts pointed toward each other. You want to be able to sense a connection between the base of your spine, through your heart, to the top of your head. And from your heart to your Beloved's heart.

On the pillow, both of you place your left hands palm up, and your right hand palm down onto your Beloved's right hand. Let your hands be relaxed and softly connected.

Old things are done away, and all things have become new.

Close your eyes and count slowly (silently) from one to nine. While you are counting, notice your body relaxing. Feel how the chair or floor supports your body. Notice when your breathing changes, without trying to control it.

After reaching the count of nine, allow your eyes to slowly open. Whether or not your Beloved's eyes are also open, gaze upon your Beloved, making eye contact when their eyes also open. Once both of you establish eye contact, remain in that joyous connection for a few moments or as long as feels comfortable. Allow your Beloved to see into your soul through your eyes, while you continue to breathe and feel the support of the floor and/or your chair. Let your attention move between the different sensations in your body.

When you are ready to close your eyes again, say out loud to the other, "I am here." Wait a moment for the words to settle into the atmosphere. When we speak from a meditative space, the words resound in our hearts. Listen and feel the effect of these words. Then, the other responds, "I am here." "I am here" is very powerful; so is "I love you," "I will always be here," or "I am with you in spirit." After a moment, both of you will close your eyes again for nine counts.

If, therefore, thine eye be single, thy whole body shall be full of light.

Then each say any or each of the following:

Thank you for being in my life.

Thank you for looking into my eyes.

Thank you for being here with me right now.

Thank you for being present.

Thank you for everything you do for me.

Thank you for warming my heart.

Thank you for allowing me to love you.

Thank you for hearing me.

Thank you for sharing this moment.

Thank you for being you.

Thank you for allowing me to be me.

Thank you for growing with me.

Thank you for seeing me.

Thank you for touching me.

Thank you for loving Christ.

When you are ready to end the meditation, each of you places your own hands palms together (prayer position) and holds them in front of your own heart center (center of your chest area). Continuing eye contact, you bow slightly to each other. Bowing this way honors the Spirit in one another and your shared joy.

Behold, thou art my people.

CHAPTER EIGHT

Evening, and morning, and noon,
I meditate, and make a noise,
and He heareth my voice.

—*Psalms 55;17*

SPIRITUAL PSYCHOLOGY

For the Western student of meditation, it is useful to examine spiritual or transpersonal psychology. This is branch of psychology has to do with inner experiences that go beyond one's personal experiences or issues, although those personal experiences or issues may well be part of the transcendent experience. Because its terms and models are drawn from Western psychology, transpersonal psychology, which often focuses on meditative ideas and experiences, can be quite useful to the Western student of Eastern practices.

This theoretical base has been useful to me as a psychologist, because it helps me help clients who may not have a specific religious belief or who may be struggling with one. Transpersonal psychology, in short, can be

I have taken out of thy hand the cup of trembling; thou shalt no more drink it again.

spiritually beneficial to anyone, in any faith tradition or lack of faith tradition, to access the Divine in unique and immediate ways. This personal access to the Divine certainly nurtures faith (if one already has a faith commitment), helps one find a way to faith, or even help someone who is agnostic discover important spiritual insights and have rich spiritual experiences.

Know ye not that I, the Lord your God, have created all men.

A fundamental aim of transpersonal theory is (as its name indicates) to transcend the merely personal in order to find a reality that is higher and more lasting than could ever be found within the narrow boundaries of the limited self. Whereas in most conventional forms of counseling, a person is encouraged to make and celebrate his or her biographical narrative as the ultimate project, the transpersonal therapist says that there is yet another project after the biographical one has reached its limit. This project is concerned not so much with our stories as with fear and attachment and their release, and with bringing mindfulness to areas of delusion, grasping, and unnecessary suffering. One can, at times, find the deepest realizations of self and non-attachment through some of the methods of transpersonal psychology.

To reach this supra-individual "disidentification" from the issues that had heretofore defined one's "self," transpersonal theorists insist upon the need for some form of meditative practice, which have been called the "royal road to the transpersonal."

One of the most immediate effects of regular meditative practice—and one which is a central objective of transpersonal therapy—is what the early transpersonal psychiatrist Roberto Assagioli called "disidentification from sub-personalities." Ferrucci, a follower of Assagioli, explains:

"One of the most harmful illusions that can beguile us is the belief that we are an indivisible, immutable, totally consistent being…. We can easily perceive our actual multiplicity by realizing how often we modify our general outlook, changing our model of the universe with the same facility with which we change dress. Our varying models of the universe color our perception and influence our way of being. And for each of them we develop a corresponding self-image, and a set of body postures and gestures, feelings, behaviors, words, habits, and beliefs. This entire constellation of elements constitutes in itself a kind of miniature personality, or, as we call it, a subpersonality. Subpersonalities are psychological satellites, coexisting as a multitude of lives within the overall medium of our personality. Each subpersonality has a style and a motivation of its own, often strikingly dissimilar from those of others. Each of us is a crowd. There can be the rebel and the intellectual, the seducer and the housewife, the organizer and the *bon vivant*. Often they are far from being at peace with each other."

I give unto you to be the light of this people.

Exercise #1

Ye shall have great joy and be exceedingly glad.

Imagine that you are in a high mountain meadow. It is summer; the air is clean and clear; and the sun is bright, but not hot. You are free. Smell the air, notice the wildflowers, hear the small stream that runs through the meadow… breathe…. As you look around you see that someone is coming to join you. See who that is. Be with that person…breathe…. Now notice that the meadow is ringed by mountains. Choose one you would like to climb. Gather what you need and begin the ascent with the person who joined you.

Be aware of your hands, feet, the feeling of the rocks. When you've climbed about 1/3 of the way up the mountain, you come to a ledge. Standing on the ledge is an old woman. Look at her. She has something to give you for the journey. Tell her, "Thank you," and continue climbing.

Continue the climb up the mountain. About 2/3rds of the way, you come to another ledge. Climb up on it. Standing there is an old man, who has something to tell you about the rest of the climb. Listen to what he has to say, the continue on the climb to the top.

Once you reach the top. Look around and feel what it feels like to reach the top. As you look around, you will see that the sun moves slowly toward you, toward the top of the mountain. You do not have to worry—it is is not any hotter or brighter. When it reaches the top, look into the sun and see that there is a door. Leave your climbing partner behind and step through the door to the other side.

Once through to the other side, you will be met by a guide. See who that is and embrace or shake hands. The guide will now lead you down into an idyllic valley. You see small houses, animals, people wandering about. He/she takes you to a spacious building in the middle of the valley.

You now enter the beautiful building, and your guide leads you down a long hall. At the end of the hall, he/she opens a door. Seated in the room on the other side of the door is a group of wise beings at a table. You sit down on the opposite side of the table and take in their faces. You have the opportunity to ask any question you would like to ask, and they will answer. (Take time to allow questions to emerge and to listen for the answers.)

Arise and come forth unto me, that ye may thrust your hands into my side.

Old things are done away, and all things have become new.

When you are done, your guide takes you back down the hall, out into an idyllic scene and up to the door of the sun. Again hug or shake hands with your guide and step back onto the mountain top. You are joined by the your climbing partner. Stop and feel how you feel now that you have come back from the sun. Then make the climb back down to the meadow and look back up to review what happened in your journey. Record your impressions.

Each of the characters that you encountered are example of your sub-personalities. The wise, nurturing old woman is the aspect of yourself that nurtures and provides for life's basics. The wise, old man is that part that knows about how the world works. The guide is the part of you that has paranormal and spiritual impulses. The wise beings are those parts who can help bring you to reside in a higher state of consciousness.

Attaining a sense of the illusory nature of the self by watching one's many selves rise and fall in consciousness during a meditation session is the crucial first step in dispelling the illusion that there ever was or ever could be a fixed, immutable "conscious self" in the first place. To grasp this fact is "to go transpersonal." One trains the mind to observe the rising and falling of "subpersonalities" with detachment. This leads to greater emotional presence and practical efficiency.

The therapeutic possibilities of managing psychic pain through objective detachment are enormous. Again Ferruci: "When we recognize a subpersonality, we are able to step outside it and observe it. [This is] disidentification. Because we all have a tendency to identify with—become one with—this or that subpersonality, we come implicitly to believe that we are it. Disidentification consists of our snapping out of this illusion and returning to our Self. If is often accompanied by a sense of insight and liberation."

That which recognizes and peacefully observes all of the different subpersonalities spinning around it like planets around a sun, but which is not itself a subpersonality, is called the Observing Self. In a related metaphor, the Observing Self could be seen as a neutral hub of mere observation around all the spokes of the sub-personalities go round and round. Since it observes all the sub-personalities as an organizing center of our consciousness but is not itself any of those sub-personalities, it is, in a sense, "empty." But of course, this is not mere vacancy. Rather, it is a non-attachment to things which, because it is non-attached, sees clearly. It could (and often is) also called "transcendent" because it goes above the limitations of a personal view of things to view everything from this eternal, universal "center" that is in each of us.

At the end of John's Gospel, the Lord promises to give us peace. We believe that a certain measure of that peace refers to this Observing Self, which, aware of the eternal reality and sovereignty of Jesus Christ both in our souls and

I am the real vine and my Father is the gardener.

in history, does not to allow itself to get too attached to our personal victories and losses. When we rest in the eternal calm of the center, which watches all things rise and fall with detachment, and know that Jesus is the master choreographer of all of these dances of our sub-personalities, we may experience more of what the Lord promises at the end of John's Gospel when he says, "Peace is my parting gift to you. Not as the world gives do I give unto you."

Behold and lo, the Bridegroom cometh; go ye out to meet him.

Freed from the painful illusion of separation and able to witness—instead of suffer—the reality of impermanence, the Observing or Transpersonal Self now begins to intuit that it is connected to a Reality that goes beyond, even above, ego and time. Indeed, at the farthest reaches of this experience, consciousness comes to know not only that it is related to this. Reality beyond time, space and ego, but that, ultimately and eternally, it is this Reality. This is the Hindu realization: Thou art the Divine.

For the experience of the transpersonal to be durable, healing, and life-altering, occasional "peak experiences," as we meditate, are not enough. This may be difficult because of the almost literally "entrancing" nature of some of those peak experiences, which exert such a tremendous power to fascinate that they can easily become ends in themselves. Such experiences include the well-documented existence of paranormal, psychic and synchronistic events that begin not only to occur on this landscape but even to abound. Some transpersonal scholars and practitioners seem quite content to rest in this territory of spiritual manifestations as sufficient—the end of the journey. Most spiritual psychologists, however, see these manifestations as, at best, only part of the complete spiritual story; some even dismiss such things as more or less distractions on the road to complete enlightenment; others, including myself, see them as necessary and valuable but secondary stepping stones on the road to the highest states of consciousness. In short, these phenomena—or *siddhis*, as they are called in Hinduism—are not nearly as important as a vision of the Whole which infuses one's entire life, not just rare and exciting moments. The fruit of such vision is compassion and virtuous living for the benefit of all sentient beings. This experience of and identification with the Self is what we as Christians recognize, in its highest and truest form, as being what St. Paul was talking about when he wrote, "Not I live, but Christ within me." When one has found the living Christ within oneself, one has, I believe, found what St. Paul is talking about and the highest instance of what transpersonal theory calls the Self. To live from that sacred inner point of "Christ within" should be every Christian's goal, of course.

One sees these views in the writings of Christianity's greatest mystics: for instance, Hildegard of Bingen and Teresa of Avila.

Hildegard says that she first saw "The Shade of the Living Light" at the age of three, and by the age of five she began to understand that she was experiencing visions. In Hildegard's youth, she referred to her visionary gift as her *viso*. She explained that she saw all things in the light of

Look and I will show you the world for the space of many generations.

God through the five senses: sight, hearing, taste, smell, and touch. Hildegard was hesitant to share her visions. Throughout her life, she continued to have many visions, and in 1141, at the age of 42, Hildegard received a vision she believed to be an instruction from God, to "write down that which you see and hear." Still hesitant to record her visions, Hildegard became physically ill.

Lazarus, come forth.

In her first theological text, *Scitivas* ("Know the Ways"), Hildegard describes her struggle within: "But I, though I saw and heard these things, refused to write for a long time through doubt and bad opinion and the diversity of human words, not with stubbornness but in the exercise of humility, until, laid low by the scourge of God, I fell upon a bed of sickness; then, compelled at last by many illnesses, and by the witness of a certain noble maiden of good conduct [the nun Richardis von Stade]…I set my hand to the writing. While I was doing it, I sensed, as I mentioned before, the deep profundity of scriptural exposition; and, raising myself from illness by the strength I received, I brought this work to a close—though just barely—in ten years. And I spoke and wrote these things not by the invention of my heart or that of any other person, but as by the secret mysteries of God I heard and received them in the heavenly places. And again I heard a voice from Heaven saying to me, 'Cry out therefore, and write thus!'"

In psychology we have a term for that resistance to God's call: it is called the Jonah complex. When we finally land on the beaches of Nineva, we are relieved to do as He commands.

So Hildegard wrote. Here is an example: "And my soul ascends in this vision, as God wills, to the height of the firmament…and extends itself to many different peoples who live far from me in distant lands and spaces…. The light I see is not local; it is far, far brighter than the cloud that carries the sun. And I cannot see depth or length or breadth in it…. And as sun, moon, and stars are reflected in the water, so in this light the images of the writings and the speech and the forces and many works of men shine forth to me…. And the words in this vision are not like the words that sound from the mouths of human beings, but like a vibrating flame and like a cloud moving in pure air…and what I see and hear in that vision, my soul draws up as from a spring that still remains full and unexhausted."

Blessed are the peacemakers; they shall be called God's children.

From Teresa of Avila we read about her inner dialogue with Christ: "(The soul) should imagine itself to be in the presence of Jesus Christ, to talk with Him often, and to fall in love for His Humanity, keeping it always alive within. It should ask Him for help in times of need, weep with Him in times of need, weep with Him in pain, and be careful not to forget Him in prosperity, and all this has to be done not with contrived orations: it should be expressed in simple words, in tune with one's wishes and needs. This is an excellent method for reaping great benefits in a short time."

And the anonymous Russian Pilgrim, a nineteenth-century mystic, repeated the name of Jesus as he breathed, concentrating on his heart. This ancient technique, taken from the teachings of the Philakalia, was supposed to be used throughout the day. As he breathed in, the pilgrim would say "Lord Jesus Christ," and as he breathed out, he would say, "Have mercy on me."

He wrote: "Sometimes my understanding, which had been so stupid before, was given so much light that I could easily grasp and dwell upon matters of which up to now I had not been able even to think at all. Sometimes that sense of a warm gladness in my heart spread throughout my whole being, and I was deeply moved as the fact of the presence of God everywhere was brought home to me. Sometimes by calling upon the Name of Jesus I was overwhelmed with bliss, and now I knew the meaning of the words, 'The Kingdom of God is within you.'"

Exult and be glad, for you have a rich reward in heaven..

Lectio Divina Exercise

Many of us have read the Serenity Prayer of St. Francis of Assissi which begins, "Lord, make us the instrument of Thy peace." There is a way to really access the deeper meaning of the prayer—through *lectio divina*. A very ancient art, practiced at one time by all Christians, it is slow, contemplative praying of a spiritual passage which enables it to become a means of union with God.

1. Reading/listening – the art of *lectio divina* begins with cultivating the ability to listen deeply, to hear "with the ear of our hearts." We should allow ourselves to become women and men who are able to listen for the still, small

voice of God (I Kings 19:12); the "faint murmuring sound" which is God's word for us, God's voice touching our hearts. This gentle listening is an "atunement" to the presence of God in that special part of God's creation which is the Scriptures. The reading or listening which is the first step in *lectio divina* is very different from the speed reading which modern Christians apply to newspapers, books and even to the Bible. *Lectio divina* is reverential listening; listening both in a spirit of silence and of awe. We are listening for the still, small voice of God that will speak to us personally—not loudly, but intimately. In *lectio divina* we read slowly, attentively, gently listening to hear a particular word or phrase.

You are the light for all the world.

2. As we read St. Francis' prayer very slowly, we should find a word or a phrase that speaks to us in a personal way and "ruminate" on it. The image of the ruminant animal quietly chewing its cud was used in antiquity as a symbol of the Christian pondering the Word of God. Christians have always seen a scriptural invitation to *lectio divina* in the example of the Virgin Mary "pondering in her heart" what she saw and heard of Christ (Luke 2:19). Then we should memorize it and while gently repeating it, allow it to interact with our thoughts, hopes, memories, desires.

3. The third step in *lectio divina* is prayer. In this exercise we allow the word that we have taken in and on which we are pondering to touch and change our deepest selves. God invites us in *lectio divina* to hold up our most difficult and pain-filled experiences to Him, and to gently recite over

them the healing word or phrase. In this way, we allow our real selves to be touched and changed by the word of God.

4. Finally, we simply rest in the presence of the One who has used His word as a means of inviting us to accept His transforming embrace. No one who has ever been in love needs to be reminded that there are moments in loving relationships when words are unnecessary. It is the same in our relationship with God. Wordless, quiet rest in the presence of the One Who loves us, helps us enjoy the experience of being in the presence of the Lord.

Come ye near unto me.

St. Francis' Prayer

Lord, make us the instrument of Thy peace
Where there is hatred, let us sow love
Where there is injury, pardon
Where there is doubt, faith
Where there is despair, hope
Where there is darkness, light
Where there is sadness, joy
May we seek not so much to be consoled as to console
Not so much to be understood as to understand
Not so much to be loved as to love
For it is in giving that we receive
It is in pardoning that we are pardoned
It is in dying that we awake to eternal life.

CHAPTER NINE

The flowering of love is meditation.
—*J. Krishnamurti*

FAMILY MEDITATION

As we work toward the ideal of eternal family, we often fall into fits of despair about how we can help our family deal with anger, resentment, impatience, negative attitudes toward self and family members. We ask, Where is the peaceful, loving family I imagined? Many times we struggle with what to do to gather family closer together—how to blend age, attention span and interests.

Meditation is something we can introduce easily and produces the early result of better moods, less stress and anxiety. As parents we teach our children to care for their bodies by eating nutritiously and getting enough sleep, but we are not quite as clear when it comes to teaching them how to maintain their interior equilibrium. Extensive research confirms that just a few minutes of sitting meditation each day calms the mind, body and spirit. When family

Great shall be the peace of thy children.

members have a peaceful place inside themselves, they naturally become happier and more positive, getting along better with each other and those in their world. For both children and adults, everyday obstacles become more workable and natural harmony is easily regained. Children experience an open heart; our patience becomes authentic patience. We are no longer gritting our teeth, trying to be patient. We feel the timelessness of each moment and actually are patient. We feel like offering unconditional attention, unconditional time.

Behold your little ones.

Before Meditation

Create a clean, quiet space where the family will meditate. I suggest that you place a picture of the Lord in the area where He can be seen by all. Some people like to place flowers or light a candle. If the family uses chairs, place the same chair, same place in the room for everyone. Our body grows accustomed to routine, particularly in this instance. If you or the children would like to sit on a cushion on the floor, you can sit on folded blankets or purchase round pillows or *zabutons* online. A timer is very helpful, so that you can relax and meditate without having to be aware of time. Some people like to use a bell or gong to start the session.

Passive Meditation

Young children can benefit from several minutes of passive meditation, even though they may not sit perfectly still. They are very sensitive and will benefit from the sensations of the family in meditation, since they naturally soak up the peace in the atmosphere.

Beginning with breath, have the older children and parents do the in-six, hold-six, out-breath routine mentioned earlier. For the younger ones, have them do three in, etc. (The body responds to patterns of three.) When everyone is in a quiet frame of mind, then go back to your posture with head and shoulders held up, spine straight. Close your eyes. Find your own "seat." Feel energy move up your energy. Feel the strength of the earth beneath you, the sky above you, and your own heart, body and mind bridging them together, joining heaven and earth.

At first we need to take stock in just where we are at the moment. The natural speed with which we operate is such that when we first stop, we spin around and around in our thoughts. So we need to take the time to settle down and become present with ourselves and see who we are at that particular moment.

Then gently bring your attention to your natural breathing rhythm. Feel the air going in and out of your nose; feel your chest rising and falling. Pay more attention to the out-breath than the in-breath. When we just flow out with the expansive quality of our out-breath, then we let go of our thoughts. Rest your mind in that space for a moment before breathing back in. When you breathe back in, try imagining that you are breathing in the Spirit, filling you with peace and joy.

Pray in your families unto the Father.

As suggested in earlier chapters, counting the in-breath or saying a phrase over and over in one's mind helps keep the busy mind at bay. Common phrases are: Be still and know that I am God; Peace, be still; Abba, Father; Thy will be done; I am in your midst, and Filled with the love of God.

Go thy way; thy son liveth.

After a five-minute session, have each family member report on their success at quieting their "monkey mind." Then the little ones can be excused to read or do some quiet activity out of earshot.

Walking Meditation

Another activity that the whole family can do together is the walking meditation exercise detailed in Chapter Six. Have the little ones head the line. They help everyone else walk in a slower, more deliberate fashion.

Remind the family that, as they walk, they should be trying to let go of their thoughts. But it is not easy—we have to do it over and over again—a bit like training your new puppy to sit. We have to be gentle about it, but determined, too. And it is important not to judge our thoughts. They are not inherently good or bad—in the end, they are just thoughts. We do not necessarily act on them. They are just thoughts. Let them go. As soon as we realize, "Oh, I'm thinking…" —whatever it is, you can gently acknowledge that it is just a thought. Just let it go, whatever it is, and bring your attention back to the present.

Active Meditation

Parents should be ready with a visualization exercise, such as the Lord descending to stand in front of a family member. You can ask to see if there are favorites, like the ascent into the sun or the practice of compassion meditation. These exercises can be repeated, as our imagination is endless in its originality. You can also, of course, think of guided imagery to suit the family's circumstances.

Once the exercise is over, divide the group into twos and have each describe their experience. (Mom or Dad can opt out if there is an odd number.) When the group is reassembled, have each member chose one word to describe how they feel at the moment.

Then have the group stand in a circle, right hand over left and quietly send energy from the left hand to the right. Invite Christ into the center of the family circle. Ask that the

For can a woman forget her sucking child, that she should not have compassion on the son of her womb?

Spirit follow each person throughout the day. Hugging each other at the end cements the experience.

Mandala Exercise

The *mandala* is a square within a circle that used for meditation in Tibetan Buddhism. Westerners have taken the *mandala* and used it to express their inner sense of self.

I can of mine own self do nothing.

As a family exercise, it is fun and eye-opening to see how everyone sees themselves. Have crayons ready. Ask each member of the family to color, and if they want to, write a word or phrase in each of the following areas: In the middle, the center circle represents the soul.

The petals around the circle are aspects of self, such as friend, mother, sister, dancer, businessman, etc. The rest of the design is a courtyard with steps going up to the center. At the entrance to each staircase, there is a guardian. Write or draw who guards your inner world. Finally there are rings around the square. These are energy "rings" or psychic protection for our soul. Color these or make a design with this pattern.

When everyone is done, have them explain what has been produced and then hang these mandalas, so people can be effected by the creative and spiritual statements made.

True worshippers shall worship the Father in spirit and truth.

I AM Poem

One of the interesting exercises for a family is the I AM poem. Members express what they think about themselves in a structured poem that lets everyone sound like a seasoned poet. This is an exercise for the older children. When the poems are finished, have members read them aloud.

I Am

1st Stanza:

I am (two special characteristics you have)

I wonder (something you are actually curious about)

I hear (an imaginary sound, not some sound in the room)

I see (an imaginary sight)

He will show him greater works than these, that ye may marvel.

I want (an actual desire)

I am (repeat the first line of the poem)

2nd Stanza

I pretend (something you actually pretend to do)

I feel (a feeling about something imaginary)

I touch (imaginary touch, not something you are actually touching)

I worry (something that really bothers you)

I cry (something that makes you very sad)

I am (repeat the first line of the poem)

3rd Stanza

I understand (something you know to be true)

I say (something you believe in)

I dream (something you actually dream about)

I try (something you really make an effort to do)

I hope (something you actually hope for)

I am (repeat the first line of the poem)

For Younger Children

If your family is composed of younger children, here are a few suggestions to appeal to their age and activity level. First, the walking meditation is ideal. Any visualization, like the ones in Chapter Ten, where there is a beginning of a story, and they are left to finish the story is very good. Visualizations, like the ones where Christ descends from above, are also good.

Search the scriptures; for in them ye think ye have eternal life.

Kirtan Exercise

The kirtan meditation involves the chanting of primal sounds that signify the stages of life. They are: *Sa*, which means birth, *Ta*, life or existence, *Na* which means death, and *Ma*, which we would call resurrection.

Along with the chanting, one touches fingers together with each sound. On *Sa*, touch the index fingers of each hand to your thumbs. On *Ta*, touch your middle fingers to your thumbs. On *Na*, touch your ring fingers to your thumbs. On *Ma*, touch your little fingers to your thumbs.

For two minutes, chant in your normal voice, or "voice of action" —so called by the yogis; then for next two minutes, chant in a whisper, which is called the "voice of the lover. For the next three minutes, chant silently, which is called the "divine language."

Then reverse the order, whispering for two minutes and chanting the mantra out loud for two minutes, for a total of eleven minutes.

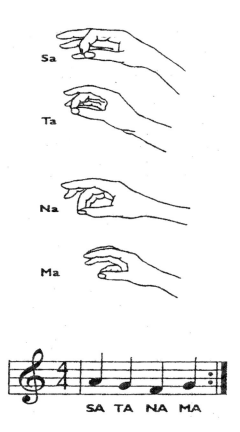

Wherefore, go to, thy faith hath made thee whole.

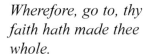

Benefits of Meditation for the Family

1. When you, as parents, have slowed down and are paying closer attention to the immediate world, you will see things that you ordinarily might not notice. And you can feel things you could not feel before. Then you communicate better in a more relaxed and open way.

2. When the family all feels the sense of timelessness when they have been meditating together, a sense of humor

and sense of peace emerges, which helps everyone feel kinder, gentler and patient.

3. As I noted earlier, the left prefrontal lobe is where positive feelings are generated. To generate an uplifting energy from the meditative experience gives one the means to work out even the most challenging of experiences in the family. This vibrant energy springs from that natural buoyancy we all have when we are not consumed with mental and emotional baggage that runs around in our conscious mind.

4. For your children, there are a number of benefits: a) They become sure of who they are and can therefore stand their own ground, confident and open; b) They are not afraid to stand up for their beliefs and do the right thing, because they are comfortable with who they are; and c) They can calm themselves and deal with situations that confront them in this increasingly neurotic world, and 4) They report that they feel closer to their siblings and parents.

5. The presence of the Lord is more evident whenever the family gathers in His name, evokes the Spirit and quietly enters into the pure silence that meditation can bring.

Man is not to live on bread alone, but on every word that comes from the mouth of God.

CHAPTER TEN

My meditation of him shall be sweet:
I will be glad in the Lord.

—Psalms 104:34

DREAMS AND MEDITATION

As soon we sit down, quiet our mind and rest from the "monkey chatter," we become aware of deeper thoughts and feelings, ones that seem to surface mostly from our dream state.

Each person's unique history produces a unique set of conscious and subconscious issues in that person. And each human being—like any living organism—innately possesses certain fundamental ways of experiencing, understanding, and acting in the world and on it. These inborn perspectives and predispositions, which preceded individual experience, are more deeply embedded in the individual's psyche than his merely personal subconscious. Indeed, they are the primal bedrock upon which both the conscious and subconscious mind subsequently develop from birth to

The Lord will go before you, and the God of Israel shall be your rearward.

*With great mercies
will I gather thee.*

death. We come hardwired with these basic ways of seeing and interpreting the world. These specie-specific ways of seeing and being exist not in a personal subconscious but in a collective unconscious—"collective" because it is innate and similar in all human beings, "unconscious" because it existed in a much more ancient and much less accessible realm of psyche than the person's transitory and experientially conditioned subconscious. According to pioneering psychiatrist, Carl Jung, the collective unconscious consists of archetypes.

Archetypes are the primary structures and categories through which we experience and act upon both our inner and outer worlds. Archetypes both enable and constrain human knowledge. They enable because they are the filters of human experience that allow us to understand and act on our world. They are constraining because we understand and act on our world only through these filters. What we experience is not necessarily reality as such, and certainly not reality in its totality, but simply the version of it that filters through the archetypes.

Much of the meditative process is an attempt to move through or around these archetypes to a clear, higher state of consciousness. But first, we must be aware of archetypes that are activated in our unconscious in order to engage them productively. They are readily accessed if we remember our dreams. A certain portion of our dreams are archetypal in that they contain these primary symbols.

Examples of archetypal narrative patterns include: the hero's/ heroine's journey through a forest or desert of trials; the dethroning of an old king and enthroning of a new, young one—often accompanied by the restoration of the kingdom; the sacrificial death and resurrection of a savior-god—also accompanied by the restoration of the kingdom; the struggle of a young man and woman to marry against some great odds—often the result of certain social sanctions. Some of the most important archetypes of persons or animals include: king, queen, trickster, lover, bride and groom, wise one/teacher, disciple, divine child, eternal child, magical helpful animal, dragon/leviathan, the nurturing mother, the witch, harlot/temptress, Amazon, psychic/medium, law-giving father, evil king, rogue, warrior, negative old man, devil, and savior.

My meat is to do the will of him that sent me, and to finish his work.

Archetypal events include: birth, baptism, initiation, education, vocation, courtship, matrimony, ritual sacrifice, death, and final judgment. Some of the most prominent archetypal landscapes and structures are the wilderness, city, home, place of instruction, temple, battlefield, heaven and hell.

Certain geometrical shapes are also prominent not only cross-culturally in art and religion but in dreams: circles, squares (especially crosses) and triangles (especially in three-person godheads). Certain numbers also seem to have particularly profound psychological and spiritual significance and are therefore probably of archetypal import: one signifying unity; two, duality; three, the reconciliation of tension in a new (i.e., third) perspective which unites but transcends the opposing polarities; and four, the creation of a new foundation upon which the new perspective can become established. The prime numbers also seem to have particular psycho-spiritual significance.

Although it is impossible to experience an archetype directly, it is possible to access, experience, work with, and to a certain extent "understand" archetypes in an indirect but still enormously compelling manner because archetypal energy manifests itself in the form of archetypal images and symbols. The archetype in its basic state can never be immediately understood or experienced, but its symbolic manifestations can. The situation is analogous to that of wind creating patterns in the sand. We cannot see the wind that creates various figures in the sand but, since we do see the figures, we can infer various things about the basic structure and dynamics of the shaping wind by analyzing its varied sandy traces.

Ask and you will receive, that your joy may be complete.

Exercise #1

This is an active meditative exercise that would allow you to experience an archetypal symbol. Sit with your back straight and take two long breaths (6 in 6 counts, hold 6, out 6). Read aloud one of the following:

1. A frog jumps out of pond and onto my lap and croaks, "I am here."

2. A bird builds a nest in my hair.

3. I am in Australia when a large kangaroo grabs me and puts me in her pouch.

4. I are walking down a street in an old English town. I pass an abandoned house and from within, I hear a baby cry.

5. I wake up in the house I grew up in when I was very young. I go to the mirror to discover that I have become my own mother and I realize it is time to wake up the child that is me.

6. A strong and beautiful hand emerges from a rock which I am sitting on. I grab the hand ,and it pulls me into the rock.

7. I am fiddling with my favorite ring next to a pond. Suddenly it slips from my finger and disappears to the bottom of this murky pond. I know it will be difficult to find it, when a brightly colored snake rises out of the pond and offers to retrieve the ring if I will help him find his true home. He warns that the journey will be difficult and dangerous.

8. I am lost in the woods, in despair thinking about my life and its meaning. From behind an ancient oak tree emerges a man or woman dressed in classical Greek clothing. He/she offers to guide me through hell, purgatory, and heaven.

9. I am standing under an ancient tree when suddenly the wind begins to blow fiercely. In the branches of the tree, I hear, "Now is the time to know God." A bolt of lightning strikes the tree in the center. It splits in two, revealing a golden door.

Rise, take up thy bed, and walk.

10. I am standing before an ancient temple at dawn at the time of the full moon. On the eastern horizon, the sun in rising and on the western the moon is setting. Across the sky streaks a falling star. In that moment I understand and contain within myself the universe.

Behold, I have refined thee.

Then let your eyes float up so they are looking at a point between your eyebrows. (If you aren't sure where that is, press your finger in that location.) This activates the location where dreams are generated—the sixth level of consciousness.

From that detached position, watch as a "story" begins to unfold from this symbol. Don't censor or try to make the story into something that you necessarily want or are familiar with. It does not have to make sense. By allowing your archetypal story to emerge and being just an observer, you will eventually have control over these powerful energies. Then, if you do not get attached but simply observe them, experience them as dispassionately as possible, and then just let them go, you can flow on up to more joyful, creative and spiritual heights. Write your story in your journal. You can return to any of these images and see what may happen then. You can make your own list of stimulating images. This experience can be the source for a short story, piece of art or even a music composition.

Exercise #2

Now that you have entered this twilight world with closed eyes looking upward, move forward with this intention to explore your spiritual history. Ask about what spiritual steppingstones there have been in your life—what moments that defined your spiritual self. Wait in quiet receptivity. Accept whatever comes up—emotional feelings, sensory impressions, memories, even metaphors. Write each down as they emerge. Do not try to make this chronological. Ask yourself silently, "Where in my lifetime have events occurred that have defined me as a spiritual being?"

Sit as long as there seems to be images and memories. Then, limiting your list to twelve entries, write down a paragraph of memories of each entry. Next list these events chronologically. Ask yourself what pattern or patterns can you see with this list. Read aloud what you have written. Allow yourself to imagine what will follow—as you search for meaning in your life.

This is a great exercise for couples. To share at these depths is a chance for a deep, intimate bonding.

My right hand hath spanned the heavens.

CHAPTER ELEVEN

To open their eyes and to turn them
from darkness to light,
and from the power of Satan
unto God.

—Acts 26:18

THE TROUBLE WITH THE DEVIL

The trouble with the Devil is that he and his minions often lurk in our unconscious where they plant negative thoughts and suggestions that keep us bound to the illusion that we cannot be joy-filled and in constant contact with the Holy Spirit. We assume that it has to be under extraordinary conditions that we feel that tremendous sense of well-being.

That could be farther from the truth. With just a few minutes of concentrated work, prayer and visualization of our connection with the Lord, we can clear the clouds in our consciousness that Satan has placed, and the bright sunny day within is ours.

We are familiar with the idea that heavy drinkers, smokers, drug users carry desires so intense that minions attach

Out of my sight, Satan!

You are not to put the Lord your God to the test.

themselves to living people in order to enjoy the vice vicariously. In fact, I was acquainted with a man, who in teens, had used so much LSD that he "saw" a pitch-black vista and was so pulled into it by demonic forces that he felt that he looked directly in the face of the Devil. After that, he swallowed everything in the medicine chest and tried to commit suicide.

But what about those who do not use drugs? We can become subjects of "possession" if we are exceptionally emotional. If we feel anger or hatred at people for no reason, we may want to examine the source. Even extreme fatigue can set us up for such a state, along with feeling drained or having a heavy sensation in our solar plexus. Emotional self-discipline is so important for this reason.

There are times when an individual is in a difficult life transition, he/she may hear a voice in their head which begins by offering complimentary teachings, then says obscene things, finally encouraging the person to commit murder or suicide. One should challenge any such information, in the name of Jesus Christ.

Many erroneous assumptions are placed in our unconscious. These mostly come from assumptions passed on from one generation to another about the nature of reality and ways of coping in this earthly realm. Others are placed there by these nefarious minions.

When we meditate, these "lies" may come up over and over, along our own negative self-talk, as we try to clear our minds and become peaceful. In order to catch these patterns, try the following:

Exercise #1

Put a pad and paper beside you. Sit quietly and allow thoughts to come up. Write down each one that involves negative thoughts about yourself and others. (You may find it surprising how many and how often they repeat themselves.) Take your time with this exercise. Sit for at least five minutes and record what comes up, even if the list ends having just a few repetitive items.Now read aloud what you have written—slowly and with awareness of what you are saying. After each statement say, "That is not true." Even if these thoughts involved someone who has harmed you, the simple statement, for instance, "I hate that guy. He's such a creep," or "She has destroyed my life," are always far too simplistic to be completely true. They come from embodied feelings without involving thought or intuition.

Pray always, that you may conquer Satan.

Next, draw a line through the ones that can be readily dismissed just by saying, "That is not true," or "That is not entirely true."

You still may have several that have an emotional charge to them. Choose one that involves another person or a character from a dream which still disturbs you as you think about it.

Place an empty chair opposite you. Imagine that the individual you are thinking about is sitting opposite you. Tell him/her what is going on in your body as you see him/her sitting opposite you. (This usually involves a tightening of the chest, stomach, arms or even legs, like you would like to run.)

"Francine, when I see you sitting over there, I feel my stomach go in knots. And I feel like I want to strangle you."

Change chairs and take a moment to settle into that character. What does it feel like in your body to "be" Francine? Usually there is a shift in how you feel in your body. Tell "yourself" how you feel as you see "yourself" sitting over on the opposite chair.

But if I cast out devils by the Spirit of God, then the kingdom of God is come unto you.

Go back and settle back into your "self." Then try this formula: Tell each other what you 1) resent about the other person, 2) what you demand, and 3) what you appreciate.

After doing this and after returning to your chair, sit for a few moments and allow thoughts to come up. Write them on your note pad.

This exercise can be done with someone who helps "direct traffic," asking you to say things to the opposite chair. If you do have someone to help, then read aloud what you wrote to him/her. If you are by yourself, read it aloud anyway.

What you are accomplishing is here is clearing your consciousness of those sub-personalities or issues that are accessible to your conscious mind. What you can expect with this exercise is to diminish the amount of negative thoughts that disturb you as you meditate.

Left on the list are things that you say to yourself or are projecting onto other people that may be being implanted by dark forces to discourage you and throw you off your path.

Exercise #2
(Don't do this exercise if it frightens you,
or you feel like it opens you to dark forces.)

We know quite a bit about how Satan and his minions work. If it has been a while since you have read C.S. Lewis' *Screwtape Letters*, I recommend reading it again. It is quite revealing.

We project onto others unfinished business that we have within ourselves. We do that with the devil also. This next exercise is meant to take back those dark elements of yourself so that you can reuse the energy for higher good.

Begin with prayer for protection. Imagine a white cloak that is placed over your shoulders by the Savior. Pull up the hood. This protects you psychically. (If you become frightened in the course of this exercise, stop and simply put your arm to the square and command all evil to depart.)

Set up the chairs as you did before. Have a "helper" direct traffic. Imagine Satan sitting on the chair opposite you. Tell him what you think of him as you see him sitting over there. Really tell him off, if you feel like it. He cannot do anything to you. Get what you have wanted to say him off your chest. Then stop and feel what you are feeling in your body.

For God sent not his Son into the world to condemn the world; but that the world through him might be saved.

Next, change chairs. Take a moment to settle into the role of Satan. Sometimes people feel stronger; a smirk comes across their face. As Satan, tell "yourself" what you/he thinks of you as he sees yourself sitting over there. This is not acting. Just say whatever comes to your mind. Notice the difference in your body.

Then change chairs. See what happens in your body when you do.

And this is the condemnation, that man loved darkness rather than light.

Usually when you return to your chair, there is a feeling of relief and release. Having met the enemy, you now know what the game is, what he is up to. If you feel like there is more to be said, address Satan again and respond to his comments about you. Then respond as Satan. By that time, you can return to your chair and make some decisions about how to deal with him. Either write those ideas down or say them to your helper.

Finally remove the chair opposite you. Take it out of the room. Sit and feel what is going on in your body now that you have removed him. Catch the thoughts that are coming up. There is often much to ponder.

Finally write down affirmations about what you are going to do with this new knowledge. Read them aloud. Give thanks to Heavenly Father for your His protection and love.

(We must also realize that there is a feminine face of evil. If you feel like this exercise did not quite take care of the concerns and feelings you have, you can put a female minion on the opposite chair.)

Exercise #3

In this exercise, we assume that we have a protective shield or aura around our body. Imagine that you can see around your body. Look for either holes in your aura or sometimes people "see" things that look like "knives" or "spears" sticking into parts of the body. These may represent stab wounds from others.

Imagine that you slowly remove each foreign object. Make sure you check your back. We get "stabbed in the back" by people sometimes.

Come ye near unto me.

Then, with your hand, run over each hole in your aura several times, imagining that you are healing the wound.

This is an exercise that can be done for someone else. You run your hand over their aura with your eyes closed, imagining that you are healing and sealing the other's aura.

We can ask the Lord to help seal us from Satan's influence.

———————

It is Satan's lie that we cannot be free of him. We can. We can call upon our Savior whenever we feel him around. Take a moment to breathe freely, slowly. Feel the delight of the open atmosphere without this extra heavy "baggage." Allow the white light of the Holy Spirit to descend and fill you. You deserve peace and the feeling of security that comes with the Lord's protection.

CHAPTER TWELVE

Of the glorious majesty of your honor,
of your wondrous works,
I will meditate.

—Psalms 145:5

CONCLUSION

When we have meditated for months, it feels as natural and necessary as breathing. We find we are far more relaxed in general, and in particular when faced the difficulties of this telestial existence. More in touch with our soul, we can let this transitory illusion be. We live in it, but we are not really immersed.

By dedicated practice of meditation you will provide for yourself ideal opportunities for experiencing personal benefits and spiritual growth. At all times, when meditating and when engaged in daily activities, cultivate awareness of yourself as a spiritual being with unlimited potential, instead of seeing and feeling yourself just as a limited human being.

The Son of Man is come to save that which is lost.

Yea, they may forget:
yet will I not forget
thee...

1. Commit to regular practice—Firmly resolve that you will meditate at least 20 minutes a day. Consider this session as a daily appointment you keep with God.

2. Choose a time that is ideal for your practice. If you meditate twice a day, early morning and late afternoon or evening are suitable times. Avoid regular practice sessions immediately after eating or when overly tired.

3. Choose a place that is comfortable and quiet, where you will not be disturbed.

4. Sit in an upright and comfortable posture. Let your breathing flow naturally after the initial 6-6-6 in-breath, hold, out-breath routine. With your eyes closed, bring your awareness to the spiritual center at a point between the eyebrows.

5. Let go of your worries. Be happy. Feel thankful for the gift of the life. Say a silent prayer. Open your heart to the Lord.

6. Practice your favorite meditation technique—counting breath, saying a spiritual phrase, imagining a white beam of light, etc. Avoid passivity, sleepiness or daydreaming.

7. When it comes time to conclude, if you have problems to solve or decisions to make, use this moment when you are centered, calm and objective to address these issues.

8. Allow yourself to have a child's mind—free, present with the moment. Remember: We cannot enter the Kingdom of God except as a little child. Then turn to the scriptures and pray with all your heart.

9. Search for synchronistic moments. By that, I mean moments when things happen simultaneously that probably could not happen by chance. I take them as signs that people on the other side of the veil are involved in my life. Just other day I was returning home from the grocery store when I suddenly decided to go to a local restaurant to eat. I have not been to there for over two years and was not really hungry for pizza, but I found myself driving there. I parked, went in, was taken to a table in an out-of-the-way area and was just about to order, when my boss walked up to my table out of the men's room. We were both astonished to see each other; he more than me, for he had come to the restaurant with a former student, at that student's suggestion, and they had just said it was too bad that I was not there to join them to add insight into the student's problem. As it turned out, I was able to help him with some information I had that my boss did not. By the way, when we exited the restaurant together, I found that I had parked right next to the student's car. Now that what I call synchronicity.

Who hath ears to hear, let him hear.

10. Laugh. Laughter allows endorphins to flow through our brain and refresh our thoughts. It frees us up from the fearful and dread-filled thoughts that plague us, even just for the moment we are laughing. The act of laughing also frees us from the illusion that we are separated from God. Satan would not have us laugh freely without some dirty joke or ridicule attached. Pure laughter is like an apple a day—it keeps the doctor away.

Then shall the righteous shine forth as the sun.

11. Unhook yourself from driven perfectionistic needs. When Christ says, "Therefore I would that ye should perfect," I would like to point out that one meaning of the Greek word, *teleios*, is used to describe a person who has become fully initiated in the rituals of a religion. In Hellenistic Judaism, it means "to put someone in the position in which he can come, or stand, before God." So pushing ourselves too hard to be perfect overshoots the mark. It is a narrow canyon that Luke Skywalker barrels down. We, like Luke, need a combination of discipline and laid-back laughter, song, dance, quiet—just the right amount of lightness to feel the Force, to open that strait gate.

12. Shun the company of lesser people—unless they are family or others that we are working to bring into the gospel's light. Stay away from scenes that do not feel just right. We should hang around with people who get us high naturally, that make us feel like that bubble—light and free—moving and bouncing toward the glorious and eternal light of God.

13. Pay attention to dreams. Dreams are the most efficient way that spiritual messages can be conveyed to us. Our conscious mind, with all its driven worries and "monkey chatter," is shut down, and we are in a receptive state to receive in symbolic form, at least, what the Lord would help us with in our life. Sleep laboratories report that one in ten dreams is predictive or precognitive, portraying something that is going to happen in your life. It is a chance to rehearse before the actual event occurs. So we can learn, anticipate

and be comforted in the night, if we will just pay attention to what is happening when we drop down into another realm of consciousness.

14. Tell your friends and family spiritual stories. When I lived in Hawaii, I made many Polynesian friends and became addicted to "talking story." I sat down for the first time the other evening with a man I know who is half-Hawaiian, and within the first two minutes we were swapping stories. Let me share with you what stories we told each other that evening.

I told him of the filming of Christ-themed film on Kauai in the winter (Kauai is the wettest place on earth and the winter is the rainy season). No one who lived there would choose that time, but that is when the film crew decided to do it. They had to build a road about a half-mile long onto a ranch, and it was so muddy that when they parked their caterpillars, they would slowly slide into each other. Some of the local construction crew said they needed to bring in a *kahuna* to bless the place, and others wanted to bless the place. When they were successful, he and the crew all knelt down to pray. He asked the Great Spirit that the elements would be changed, so that they could shoot the film without the rain interfering. And from that day forward, in the daytime, it would rain all around the filming, but not on the set. But it did rain at night. If they chose to film at night, it rained in the daytime and stopped at shooting time. I know this because my good friend was there working on the set.

Loose thyself from the bands of thy neck.

Come ye near unto me.

After laughing and marveling at God's miraculous hand in man's affairs, now my new friend told me that he had gone to visit his aunt, and when he walked into the living room, he smelled the distinct odor of a particular Hawaiian flower. Now his aunt lived in Los Angeles, not Hawaii. He sat down next to her and commented on her perfume. She said she was not wearing any perfume.

"Well, I smell Hawaiian flowers."

"Oh, that," she said.

"That was your grandmother who came to visit last night."

"But Tutu is dead."

"Isn't it wonderful that her odor lingers in the house even today?"

We can deliberately put ourselves in a "God mood," no matter what is happening in our lives, and when we do that we are lifted up and given all kinds of signs that God is very aware of us and does everything to answer our prayers while letting us experience what we covenanted to do in this life. Meditation is a door opening into the constant companionship of the Holy Spirit. May we become peaceful, compassionate people, in touch with Christ and his Gospel, is my great desire.